# UNIFORMS OF THE SS

## VOLUME 6
## WAFFEN-SS CLOTHING
## AND EQUIPMENT 1939-1945

### Andrew Mollo

Windrow & Greene

**Publisher's note**

For technical reasons it has not proved possible to reproduce the colour illustrations which appeared on p. 40 of the first edition in their original position. Additional monochrome photographs have been provided on p. 40 of this edition, and the colour illustrations will be found on the rear endpaper.

Second edition
© 1992 Historical Research Unit
Designed and illustrated by Malcolm McGregor

Published in Great Britain 1992 by
Windrow & Greene Ltd
5 Gerrard Street
London W1V 7LJ

Printed in Singapore by Craft Print Pte Ltd

A CIP catalogue record for this book
is available from the British Library.

**ISBN 1–872004–67–9**

## PREFACE

Although this volume deals with the clothing and equipment of the Waffen-SS it slightly overlaps Volume 3 in the present series, since much that was worn by the SS-Verfügungstruppe remained in use, and the change-over from SS-VT to Waffen-SS was a gradual process. First official use of the title Waffen-SS appeared in an order dated 1 December 1939,[1] but it was not until 22 April 1941 that the earlier titles (SS-Verfügungstruppe and SS-Totenkopfverbände) were finally abandoned.[2] When the first volume was published in October 1968 it was the first and only book devoted entirely to SS uniform. Four other works on the subject appeared in 1971, of which two may be claimed to be of some importance and two culled from arguable and already published sources.

With the latter works in mind it was decided to translate and collate the chronology of all available orders embracing Waffen-SS clothing, standard insignia, rank badges, and personal equipment. Access to a complete record of the orders will enable the reader to assess reasons for the introduction and withdrawal of a particular item independent of an author's interpretation. Original memoranda and conversations between Himmler and his staff concerning the development of Waffen-SS uniform during and after the war will it is hoped enliven the otherwise dry matter.

The orders are complemented by three modes of illustrations: carefully selected photographs of clothing and equipment worn by serving personnel (showing as far as possible the complete uniform); separate items of head-dress, insignia and personal equipment from the author's and other collections; and detailed technical drawings emphasising cut and details to facilitate identification of surviving examples. It could be argued that all this information will enable the less-scrupulous dealers to make better copies. Be that as it may; the more accurate and detailed the information available to the collector, the more difficult it becomes to deceive him.

A common quibble from 'pseudo experts' is that the orders don't matter because the SS men disregarded the regulations and wore what they pleased, but this is not entirely true. Until the final stages of the war the German army presented a remarkably uniform appearance. The apparent variety of dress in many photographs is not primarily due to the arbitrary choice of non-regulation items but to the ever increasing number of regulations items which could be worn concurrently. Most introductory orders end up by stating that the old pattern may be worn out. This does not mean that non-regulation uniforms were not worn, and where a non-standard article persists it has been included. However, isolated examples of personal vanity have not been meticulously noted, for they were not typical of the Waffen-SS as a whole.

Those disappointed by the omission of such items as fezzes, Italian steel helmets, etc. must bear in mind that they do not constitute standard Waffen-SS clothing, being peculiar to national formations. They will be discussed in Volume 7 in chapters dealing exclusively with the appropriate formations. The following friends have greatly contributed to the accuracy and comprehensiveness of this work by their knowledge, patience and skill: Colonel C. M. Dodkins and Philip Buss BA(Hons.) for advice, criticism and correction; Friedhelm Ollenschläger for advice and proof-reading; Malcolm McGregor for the illustrations; and Andrew S. Walker for the photography.

I am equally grateful for the generous co-operation of David L. Delich, James van Fleet, Richard Deeter, Roger Harle, and Colonel C. M. Dodkins who granted me access to their private collections and from which items loaned for use in preparing this book have proved of inestimable value.

The following museums, archives and collections have supplied photographic illustrations: Imperial War Museum, London; Wiener Library, London; Bundesarchiv, Koblenz; Süddeutscher Verlag, Germany; EGV Archive, Italy; Jost Schneider Archive; Dodkins Collection.

### Author's note to second edition

In the twenty years since the appearance of the first edition of this volume very little new information has come to light which obliges me to revise or correct the contents.

Whereas the pioneering research on Waffen-SS uniform was undertaken in the United Kingdom, with generous help from American collectors, today it is the French who seem to be producing the most interesting work. Articles on various aspects of SS clothing and equipment, with special emphasis on items worn in the various campaigns in France, appear regularly in *Militaria* magazine. Detailed work has been done on Waffen-SS camouflage clothing which suggests that the difference in camouflage patterns reflected the date of manufacture; whereas one leading French expert on camouflage clothing is of the opinion that the patterns printed on waterproof duck were produced concurrently by different factories. Since no documentary evidence has been produced to support either hypothesis we do not yet know the answer.

While going through my correction copy I was reminded of the meticulous editing work carried out by Alan Kent, who — when asked to cast his highly professional eye over a copy of this volume — pointed out more battered letters, floating footnotes and typographical errors than I wish to bring to the attention of readers of this revised edition.

In conclusion, I would like to point out that Hugh Page Taylor wrote the introduction and the unit histories for Volume 3 of this series, a fact inadvertently omitted from the revised edition due to a printer's error.

Andrew Mollo
Sagonne, 1992

**CONTENTS**                                                          Page

# INTRODUCTION

The expansion of the SS at the end of 1939, from an armed political police force, to what was in reality to become a fourth branch of the armed forces was achieved against the resistance not only of the conservative and well-established armed forces, but Hitler and his Party as well. Both camps had reasons to fear a powerful, independent, and experienced armed force in their midst. But the SS had its own internal problems to overcome before it could have presented any sort of threat. Primarily a political organisation, it lacked fundamental military experience, despite the fact that many of its senior leaders, like Dietrich, Berger, and Pohl, had First World War military experience. Its military commanders – like Hausser, who had actually been a general officer in the Reichswehr before joining the SS – were few and far between. Despite an efficient officer training programme the SS was still, at the outbreak of war, desperately short of field commanders and staff officers.

The SS expressed disdain and even ridicule for the German army and its conservatism, but was nevertheless forced to call on it not only for its heavy weapons and specialised training, but also for its clothing and personal equipment. The pre-war SS Clothing Works and Depots, together with the RZM, were quite capable of supplying an Allgemeine-SS unit with a few pairs of black breeches or twenty pairs of collar patches for newly enrolled members, but was unable to supply the SS-Totenkopf-Division with 15,000 sets of clothing and equipment.

This disdain was not shared by the officer corps of the embryo Waffen-SS, many of whom had joined only because prospects of promotion were better in the SS. Their reliance on army know-how had the opposite effect of fostering an insidious process of militarisation. They prefered to use army rank titles (Leutnant instead of SS-Untersturmführer), the army salute instead of the German 'deutscher Gruss', and finally they affected army style of dress. Himmler was obliged to point out that:

## 274.  The field-grey uniform of the Waffen-SS[1].

The manufacture and method of wearing the field-grey field blouse, greatcoat and field cap of the Waffen-SS, differ widely from army regulations. They belong to the SS, as laid down by the RFSS orders of 12 December 1939 and 10 May 1940.

The collected orders in the Heeresverordnungsblättern and the Allgemeinen Heeresmitteilungen (see H.V.B1.Teil C, Blatt 26, Ziff.1007) are invalid for the Waffen-SS.I/3 1501.

Kdo.d.W.SS IVb.

and again in 1941:

## 344.  Clothing and equipment. [2]

Regulations of the OKH concerning clothing and equipment (introduction and alteration etc.) which appear in the HVBL and AHM, or in separate published orders, are invalid for the Waffen-SS.

These orders are issued to the Waffen-SS by the SS-Führungshauptamt, Kommandoamt der Waffen-SS.

Kdo.d.W.SS/Ia.

But however much Himmler resented and resisted falling in step with the army, practical considerations prevailed. For the rest of the war, this sort of announcement regularly appeared in the SS-Verordnungsblatt:

## 434.  Field-grey field uniform for crews of anti-tank guns (self propelled). [3]

The order announced in the AHM 1942, page 464, No. 893, is also valid for the Waffen-SS.

SS-FHA./Ia/i V.

But lack of experience and tradition also had its benefits. Many SS officers uninhibited by precedent set about experimenting not only with new tactics, but with suitable modern clothing and equipment with which to execute them. The German army field uniform, as worn at the beginning of the war, was only a development of that worn 70 years earlier during the Franco-Prussian war. The Waffen-SS, with their camouflage jackets and webbing equipment, would not look out of place in a modern NATO manoeuvre.

## Notes:
1. V.B1.d.W.-SS., Nr.11, 15 October 1940, Ziff. 274.
2. Ibid. Nr.16, 1 September 1941, Ziff. 344.
3. Ibid. Nr.23, 1 December 1942, Ziff. 434.

## Manufacture

Once a design or prototype had been approved, often by Himmler himself, it would be put into mass production. Manufacture would be undertaken by a private firm or one of the SS-owned economic enterprises. The first clothing works of the Waffen-SS (SS-Bekleidungswerke) was established in Dachau,[1] where almost from the beginning the SS-Verwaltungsamt had its main clothing depot (Bekleidungslager). In 1939 a works had been established in the women's concentration camp at Ravensbrück. On 1 July 1940 both these works, employing approximately 141 inmates, became part of the SS-owned company, Society for the Exploitation of Textile and Leather Goods Ltd (Gesellschaft für Textil-und Lederverwertung GmbH – Texled).[2]

Typical scene inside an SS concentration camp clothing works at the beginning of the war.

Soon new works for knitwear and straw overboots, a weaving mill, and a training school for tailors was established in Ravensbrück. By 1943 the clothing works in Dachau and Ravensbrück had achieved a very high standard, and apart from manufacturing clothing for inmates, were producing some 20% of the Waffen-SS clothing needs. Items of clothing manufactured by the SS clothing works usually bore the stamp

SS
BW

Another firm, German Equipment Works Ltd (Deutsche Ausrüstungswerke GmbH — DAW) was formed in May 1940, and operated a number of factories which undertook minor economic enterprises, including the sword smithy run by Paul Müller in Dachau from October 1939.[3]

After the occupation of Poland and parts of Russia, Eastern Industries Ltd (Ostindustrie GmbH — Osti) used Jewish inmates from concentration and labour-camps to make winter uniforms and various items of equipment from property and raw materials seized by the Germans. In October 1943 Osti took over the fur working factory attached to the forced labour camp at Trawniki, where, under the management of the German service firm of Schulz & Co, 6,000 Jews manufactured and maintained fur caps, coats, and gloves for the Waffen-SS and armed forces.

By use of KL inmates, the SS was never short of labour although increasingly short of raw materials, which necessitated restriction on the issue of new clothing and re-issue of renovated used clothing. By 1943 the shortage had become critical, and in January Pohl reported to the Reichsführer-SS: 'In the past year the situation in the field of textile and leather goods has worsened considerably.' He went on to blame this on 'the absence of supplies from abroad, the continuing expansion of the armed forces, the increase in the requirement for work clothing for foreign workers and the needs of the

**Notes:**

1. NO-678. This included a small tailors' shop established in August 1940, transferred to DAW on 1 January 1941.

2. NO-1043. The SS economic enterprises in Dachau were incorporated in DAW from 1 January 1940.

3. NO-678. The plant was opened in Dachau in February 1940, and transferred to Texled on 3 June 1940.

German civilian population as a result of general wear and tear'. After calculating the supply of raw materials available, Pohl estimated that the needs of the Waffen-SS for the year 1943 could only be met up in the following percentages:

| | |
|---|---|
| Wool | 26% |
| Cotton | 15% |
| Synthetic wool and rayon | 25% |
| Linen | 30% |
| Leather for footwear and equipment | 50% |

Pohl commented, 'This means that the wearing time of most articles must be extended by four and more'; adding, '. . . that it is only possible to ensure supplies in the long term if one exercises the utmost economy, and defers all avoidable claims from the troops. It is known, and stressed time and time again in discussions with the OKW, that compared to the army the Waffen-SS is still considerably better clothed and equipped. Our troop commanders (Truppenführer) must realise that in the fourth year of war it is no longer possible to get exceptional treatment.'

One outcome of Pohl's gloomy forecast, was Himmler's recommendation that a look out be kept for suitable foreign uniforms, but once again the SS met resistance from the army. In April 1943, SS-Gruf. Berger reported that in Denmark stocks of Danish uniforms could only be utilised (for the German army) by Commanding General von Hannecken — who was also finding difficulty in obtaining enough uniforms for German and ethnic-German conscripts. The situation was no different in December 1943, when the Höchste SS-und Polizei-Führer in Italy attempted to extract 100,000 sets of captured Italian uniforms and equipment out of the army, for use by the rapidly expanding Italian volunteer units. Although the Waffen-SS was unable to clothe 100,000 Italians from its own stocks, the army quartermaster, Oberstintendant Nierhoff at OKW/VA, played for time by saying that 'there still had not been any exact survey of available booty, and that the armed forces requirements are also very great'. He went on, 'it is therefore up to the Wehrmacht-Führungsstab to decide', and that 'a decision in writing is not to be expected before the end of the month'.

In 1943, the OKW, faced with similar problems, embarked on the next inevitable step — the standardisation of the uniform of the armed forces and organisations connected with it. In September 1940 it suggested 'that the shade and manufacture of the uniform of the Wehrmacht and the organisations connected with it should be standardised; especially as the supply situation in the field of raw materials, particularly textiles, make it increasingly difficult to keep sufficient stocks of the various colours in use, and also to further ease

Reichsführer-SS Himmler and Generaloberst Model inspect the 13th SS Volunteer Mountain Division (Croatian) on 12 January 1944. On the right is SS-Ogruf. Pohl, and behind Himmler, SS-Brigaf. Fitzhum. They all wear tailor-made greatcoats with silver grey lapels and collar patches. Himmler has a detachable fur collar.

the labour situation'. The sample of the material they sent for inspection was similar to the earth-grey that the SS-VT had used until 1937–8, and Pohl could not resist reminding Himmler that 'we realised eight years ago that this shade was undoubtedly more practical and acted accordingly. At the beginning of the war on the intervention of the OKW, we had to depart from this colour, although we were convinced that it was better'.

The OKW had to decide 'what items of uniform are to be made in future, and

in what finish. Except for naval crews, who retain their blue clothing, all units of the armed forces, Waffen-SS, Todt Organisation, Labour Corps and Red Cross, are to receive a standard uniform, identical in cut and colour.'
'The Expert Committee of the clothing industry suggests that the important requirements are introduction of a standard quality and colour of material, standard cut, standard underwear, and equipment. The remaining badges of rank and accoutrements will serve to distinguish the individual formations'.
Although discussions concerning the standardisation of uniform had taken place before the war, it was only now, in the fourth year of war, and as a result of Armament Minister Speer's pressure, that something was finally being done about it. Pohl was in favour, but doubtful of the outcome of these discussions, not knowing how the armed forces would react. He thought a decision would only be reached if Speer issued a definite order. Pohl went on to the question of the uniform of the German police, before concluding, 'we must all acknowledge that in peacetime we can have as many uniforms as we wish, but in time of war, indeed total war, we must finally and radically dispense with all our eccentricities'.
On 18th October 1943 Himmler replied that both the Waffen-SS and police endorse the standardisation of uniforms, but that he required acceptance of the earth-grey colour of our former uniforms, 'which we had to give up because of the narrow mindedness of the competent experts at the OKW'. He asked Pohl to let him know 'if my wish can be taken into account, because if it can't, I don't intend to let the matter rest there'* It was not until 8 July 1944 that Hitler inspected and finally approved the new field uniform, and authorised Speer to co-ordinate all the agencies involved in its rapid production. In fact the new field uniform arrived too late in the war to radically alter the appearance of the German soldier.

## Issue

Once manufacture had been undertaken and completion could be scheduled, an announcement appeared in the SS-Verordnungsblatt, describing the article and for whom it was intended, and instructed the field units to indent via the usual clothing channels which initially ended up at the SS-Verwaltungsamt and, after 30 January 1942 at the SS-Wirtschaft und Verwaltungs Hauptamt, Dept.B., which dealt with economic details directly related to personnel. In 1942 Dept.B was organised as follows:[1]

*This correspondence is interesting since it fails to refer to a letter from Himmler's adjutant, SS-Ostubaf. Brandt to Pohl dated 14 October 1943, which informed him that Hitler had 'forbidden the alteration of the uniform material used hitherto'.

| Amtsgruppe B : Truppenwirtschaft | |
| --- | --- |
| Amt B I | Verpflegungswirtschaft |
| Amt B II | Bekleidungswirtschaft |
| | 1. Bekl.u.Ausr.für Mann u. Führer |
| | 2. Bekleidungswerke |
| | 3. Kleiderkasse-SS |
| Amt B III | Unterkunftswirtschaft |
| Amt B IV | Rohstoffe und Beschaffung |

In principle every Waffen-SS recruit was supposed to receive a complete set of clothing and personal equipment as listed in the wartime issue schedule (Ausstattungssoll (K)), which formed part of the overall war equipment schedule (Kriegsausrüstungsnachweisung – KAN). The early schedules were quite lavish, but soon proved an unnecessary extravagance in wartime, and first to suffer reductions in basic issue, or receive inferior substitutes, were members of the Ersatz units. (See part 10.)
The following schedules for September 1940 and July 1941 list the basic issue of clothing and equipment to N.C.O.'s and men in field units.

## 45. Section IVa. ISSUE OF CLOTHING AND EQUIPMENT.[3]

Further to the order in the Verordnungsblatt der Inspektion (E)der SS-VT. Nr.2., and the summary of the relevant provisions of the Hauptamtes Haushalt und Bauten, and in order to eliminate any confusion that may still exist, we again list below articles of clothing and equipment included in the issue to N.C.O.'s and men in the event of posting to field units or transfer from one replacement unit to another:

## Obligatory Soldiers' Clothing and Equipment

| Article | Quantity |
|---|---|
| Cloth blouse, field-grey[1] | 1 |
| Cloth trousers, field-grey | 1 |
| Cloth greatcoat, field-grey[1] | 1 |
| Field cap, field-grey | 1 |
| Drill or fatigue blouse | 1 |
| Drill or fatigue trousers | 1 |
| Marching boots | 1 |
| Lace-up shoes | 1 |
| Shirt; white (or brown trikot) | 2 |
| Underpants | 2 |
| Woollen pullover | 1 |
| Balaclava helmet (Kopfschützer)[2] | 1 |
| Socks (or 2 prs. socks and 1 pr. footwraps) | 3 |
| Tie (only with brown trikot shirt)[4] | 1 |
| Neckcloth or collar liner | 2 |
| Gloves[2] | 1 |
| Pack | 1 |
| Overcoat straps | 3 |
| Mess-tin straps[3] | 2 |
| Groundsheet | 1 |
| Groundsheet pole | 3 |
| Groundsheet pegs | 3 |
| Groundsheet cord | 1 |
| Water-bottle and cup | 1 |
| Mess-tin | 1 |
| Eating utensils | 1 |
| Haversack        Haversack strap | 1 |
| Clothing bag[4] | 1 |
| Handkerchief[4] | 1 |
| Steel helmet, grey | 1 |
| Steel helmet chin strap | 1 |
| Waist belt,        Waist belt buckle | 1 |
| Bayonet frog | 1 |
| Ammunition pouches | 2 |
| Helmet cover, camouflage[4] | 1 |
| Woollen blanket (pack blanket)[2] | 1 |
| Carrying straps for tunic | 2 |
| Steel belt hooks | 4 |

Notes:
1. With appropriate insignia.
2. Only in winter.
3. Only with the old pack.
4. Only for front-line troops (Feldtruppe), if and when available.

Drivers are also to be issued with appropriate special clothing if available (except winter clothing). In the event of posting complete units to other garrisons, all clothing and equipment must accompany them.

## 348. Obligatory Clothing and Equipment for a Soldier.[4]

| Article | Quantity | Remarks |
|---|---|---|
| Cloth blouse, field-grey | 1 | With insignia |
| Cloth trousers, long, field grey (breeches for mounted personnel) | 1 | |
| Cloth greatcoat, field-grey | 1 | With insignia |
| Field cap, field-grey | 1 | |
| Drill jacket | 1 | |
| Drill trousers | 1 | |
| Marching boots (riding boots for mounted personnel) | 1 | |
| Lace-up shoes | 1 | |
| Sports shoes | 1 | Only for mounted |
| Brown, shirt, trikot[1] | 3 | |
| Underpants | 2 | |
| Woollen pullover | 1 | |
| Balaclava helmet | 1 | Only in winter |
| Socks (or 2 prs. socks and 1 pr. footwraps) | 3 | |
| Tie, black | 2 | Only with brown shirt |
| Collar liner[2] | 2 | |
| Gloves, woollen | 1 | Only in winter |
| Braces | 1 | |
| Handkerchiefs | 3 | |
| Sewing bag | 1 | |
| Cleaning brushes (set); (cleaning brush, polishing brush, clothes brush, nail brush, polish brush) | 1 | Only when absolutely necessary |
| Pack Model 34 with straps (or Pack Model 39, or combat pack with carrying straps) | 1 | Not for mounted. M.39 only when issued to units |
| Greatcoat straps | 3 | for mounted 1 only |

| | | |
|---|---|---|
| Mess-tin straps | 2 | Only with Pack Model 34 |
| Woollen blanket | 1 | |
| Groundsheet | 1 | |
| Groundsheet pole | 1 | |
| Groundsheet pegs | 2 | |
| Groundsheet line | 1 | |
| Water-bottle with cup | 1 | |
| Mess-tin | 1 | |
| Eating utensils | 1 | |
| Haversack | 1 | |
| Haversack strap | 1 | |
| Clothing bag | 1 | |
| Towel | 1 | |
| Steel helmet | 1 | |
| Steel helmet chin strap | 1 | |
| Waist belt | 1 | |
| Waist belt buckle | 1 | |
| Bayonet frog | 1 | |
| Ammunition pouch | 2 | For those equipped with a rifle. Those with small requirement, 1 pouch |
| Identity disc with cord | 1 | |
| Steel helmet cover, camouflage | 1 | Only for field units |
| Camouflage jacket | 1 | Only for field units |
| Iron ration, bag in cloth | 1 | |
| Saddle-bags, complete | 1 | Only for mounted |
| Straps supporting for ammunition pouches | 1 | Only for mounted |
| Spurs | 1 | Only for mounted |
| Spur straps | 1 | Only for mounted |
| Carrying straps for tunic | 2 | |
| Steel side hooks | 4 | |

**Notes:**

1. If a soldier is only issued with white undershirt, in place of the brown trikot shirt, he should have 2 undershirts. The undershirts are to be worn out. During the change-over from white undershirts to brown trikot shirts, brown shirts will be allocated according to the stocks of the Verwaltungsamt-SS.

2. Only with drill uniform. (See V.B1.d.W.-SS 1940., Ziff.402.) Existing neckcloths (Halsbinden) are to be included in the requirements. In the case of issue of white undershirts, the collar liner or neckcloth is to be worn with the field blouse. Neckcloths are to be worn out.
Special clothing and individual articles are to be issued according to the appropriate war equipment instructions.
The soldiers' clothing and equipment requirement as listed in the V.B1.d.W.-SS., Nr.8., 5.9.40.Ziff. 45 is hereby declared invalid.

Kdo.d.W.-SS 1Va

In January 1943 a clarification to the above order stated that:
Iron ration bag (Zwiebackbeutel) Art. No. 10392, and Fat container (Fettbüchse) Art. No. 10 442,
also constituted part of the obligatory clothing and equipment of a soldier. [4a]
The economic situation in September 1943 made it necessary to issue a newly formulated four-part schedule:

**370. Clothing Economy of the Waffen-SS.** [5]
The stock situation in the field of textiles and leather requires not only the most careful attention and maintenance of individual articles, but also significant restrictions.
For the duration of the war, therefore, a wartime issuing schedule in four parts has been established for the clothing and equipment of the Waffen-SS.
The four parts of the schedule are as follows:
Part A   for field units
Part B   for all units and offices on the home front
Part C   for tropical clothing
Part D   for additional winter clothing for units on the eastern front including Lapland and northern Norway.
Units and offices will be allocated the corresponding part of the issuing schedule.
The following is ordered for the prosecution of these measures:
1. All articles in excess of requirements are to be notified to the main office dealing with clothing economy.
2. Units and offices, which because of their special duties, are allocated two sets of clothing (blouse and trousers), shall note that those articles that are suitable for field service use, are issued only in the event of posting or for special occasions. The trousers and blouse that are not suitable for field service use, constitute training clothing (Übungsgarnitur). Usability will be determined according to strict criteria, in relation to the raw material situation.

3. In the case of Ersatz units articles of equipment are to be used only when absolutely necessary.
4. The care, completeness and proper maintenance of articles is to be supervised by the unit officers by constant clothing inspections.
5. All rules and regulations to the contrary are to be regarded as cancelled. These orders do not constitute any arbitrary action, but are measures taken in everyone's interests, and are therefore to be strictly observed.

SS-FHA/Amt IV.

As availability of clothing and equipment worsened, Ersatz units began to send replacements to the front with inferior or insufficient clothing and equipment, which impaired their fighting efficiency and imposed an added strain on the already overloaded supply situation at the front. It meant that deficiency had to be made good from unit stocks, which were never large enough to cover losses.

### 401. Completeness of equipment and clothing of drafts. [6]

The order SS-FHA, Kdo. Amt der Waffen-SS Ia of 29 January 1942 is hereby suspended.

Drafts being sent to field units are to be checked before their departure by the competent commanders and company commanders, as to the completeness of their clothing and equipment. If the required clothing and equipment cannot be issued, it is to be reported to the SS-FHA./Ia.

SS-FHA/Ia

In November 1944, further economies were effected by ceasing to issue items of clothing and equipment which could not be used during the winter months.

### 650. Equipping of troops with groundsheets and accessories as well as camouflaged drill uniforms during the winter months. [7]

From now until 15 March 1945 replacements posted to field and other units will not be equipped with groundsheets, accessories and camouflaged drill uniforms, in order to avoid the intolerable losses of these expensive items during the winter months. (See notices on the clothing economy of the Waffen-SS of the SS-WVHA – B/H – 010 geh. le.-Kr.Nr.4/44, 25 September 1944 (only received by field units).)

Replacement units and schools etc. are to use any stocks they may have for training purposes only.

Field units (divisions, brigades etc.) are to call in these items before the beginning of winter and report by telex the quantity collected to the S-WVHA – Amt B/H – Berlin – Lichterfel West, Unter de Eichen 135.

If the unit concerned is not able to preserve and store them due to local conditions or the situation, these articles are to be sent to the Waffen-SS Clothing Depot at Arolsen/Waldeck or Lieberose über Kottbus/NL. Reissue will take place in the course of the spring of 1945. SS-FHA/Ia

**Chain of supply**

A unit indents on FHA for its specific requirements. If approved FHA instructs WVHA to make the necessary issue. WVHA will then either dispatch the material direct to the unit from one of its central depots (HWL) or from the factory, or arrange for it to be made available to the unit at the nearest convenient sub-depot (TWL).

Where field formations of the Waffen-SS were likely to operate in a particular area for a considerable period, special ad hoc supply bases (Stützpunkte) were usually established at convenient points. These were small and of a temporary nature.

On the eastern front SS Supply Commands (Nachschubkommandantur)* were established as the primary link between the Hauptämter and HWLs in Germany and the sub-depots (TWL) and units in its area. A Supply Command consisted of an important group of depots administrative offices which served both as a supply base and distribution centre. It was usually commanded by an officer with the rank of SS-Oberführer. It could, subject to the approval of the local SS Economic Adviser (SS-Wirtschafter), place contracts with, or make purchases from private firms in its area. [8]

* During the planning stages the first three commands:

| | |
|---|---|
| Nordabschnitt | Riga (Latvia) |
| Südabschnitt | Krim (Crimea) |
| Mittelabschnitt | Mogilew (Western Russia) |

were known as Versorgungsstützpunkte der Waffen-SS und Polizei. Those in Latvia and Crimea were to have a clothing depot with stocks of winter and summer clothing for three divisions (30,000 men) and 10,000 policemen. The central Russian depot was to provide for two divisions and 20,000 policemen. [9]

**Notes:**

1. Soldaten wie andere auch, dok. 34, pp. 342-4.
2. Handbook of German Administration and Supply, 1944, pp. 73-80.
3. V. Bl. Insp. (E) SS-TV., Nr. 3, 1 May 1940, Ziff. 45.
4. Ibid., Nr. 16, 1 September 1941, Ziff. 348.
4a. Ibid., Nr. 2, 15 January 1943, Ziff. 30.
5. Ibid., Nr. 19, 1 October 1943, Ziff. 370.
6. Ibid., Nr. 21, 1 November 1943, Ziff. 401.
7. Ibid., Nr. 21, 1 November 1944, Ziff. 650.
8. Handbook of German Administration and Supply, 1944, pp. 73-80.
9. RF-SS Tgb.Nr.8/42 g.Kdos.

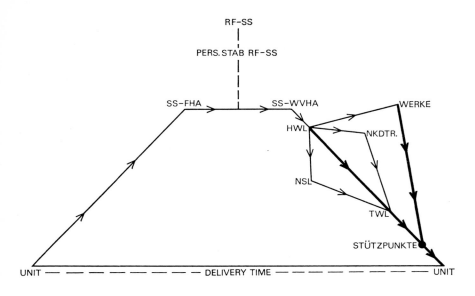

RF-SS

PERS. STAB RF-SS

SS-FHA → SS-WVHA → WERKE

HWL → NKDTR.

NSL

TWL

STÜTZPUNKTE

UNIT — — — — DELIVERY TIME — — — — UNIT

SS chain of supply.

## Purchase

In Germany, as in most European countries during the war, clothing was rationed. A newly commissioned Waffen-SS officer on leaving cadet school as either an SS-Standartenoberjunker or SS-Ustuf., received a grant towards the cost of purchasing his uniform. Before and during the first two years of the war the regular Waffen-SS officer had quite an extensive wardrobe, but later in the war most young officers purchased extra clothing only for best wear. This usually included an extra peaked and field cap, blouse, breeches, long trousers, greatcoat, gloves, belts, pistol holster, pistol, and a trunk (Mobilmachungskiste/Kleiderkoffer) the size of which varied according to rank.

Towards the cost of these items, a Waffen-SS officer received a single clothing grant (eine einmalige Bekleidungsbeihilfe) of between 350–800 RM, and the corresponding number of coupons (Uniform-Bezugscheine). Civilians entering the Waffen-SS as specialists (Fachführer) received only 250 RM, Allgemeine-SS leaders, police and officers of the armed forces received 350 RM.[1] Smaller amounts were given in the case of alteration of existing uniform, necessitated by changes in regulations.[2]

Once in possession of his clothing grant, a Waffen-SS officer was supposed to purchase his uniform requirements from one of the SS clothing counters (Kleiderkasse-SS). The SS-Clothing Counter was first established in Munich, Karlstrasse 10, in 1935, for the sale of regulation SS clothing and equipment, and in order to prevent members of the SS from having to obtain credit from their tailor for the purchase of uniforms. After the beginning of the war, the rapid provision of Waffen-SS officers with regulation clothing and equipment was also transferred to the SS-Clothing Counter. The organisation in Munich was too small for such a task, unsuitably sited, and in 1940 a bigger central sales office was opened in Berlin, although the Munich office was retained. During the war sales outlets were established in the General Government and occupied territories in order to reduce the burden on the central office, making it possible and easier for SS officers in newly occupied territories to make purchases.[3]

Use of the SS-Clothing Counter was restricted during the war to Waffen-SS, SS officers in Legions and SS formations (SS-Verbände), and to officers of the Order Police. To become a member cost 5 RM to cover administrative expenses; one then received a numbered membership card and an account number with entitlement to buy goods against payment, or arrange to have them sent C.O.D. A wartime member acquired only the right to purchase, with no further rights or obligations.[4]

The SS-Clothing Counter was administered by Hauptabteilung 3 of Amt B II in the SS-WVHA, at Berlin-Wilmersdorf, Kaiserallee 42., where its main sales outlet also was situated. The Forwarding Department was in Schlackenwerth b. Karlsbad, Sudetenland, but did not function during the war. There were eight sales points : [5]

1. Munich 33, Karlstrasse 10
2. Oslo, Ronald-Amundsen-Gate 23
3. Warsaw C I, Siegesstrasse 5
4. Lublin, Pilsudskistrasse 8a
5. Riga, Adolf-Hitler-Strasse 23
6. Kiev, Horst-Wessel-Strasse, 20
7. Prag I, Nürnberger Strasse, 27
8. Paris, Rue de Général Apper Nr.6

The SS-Clothing Counter published its own thirty-page illustrated catalogue. As in most armies during wartime, both the means and opportunity for front-line officers to kit themselves with expensive tailor-made uniforms were somewhat limited, and most relied on their unit stores to provide, against payment, issue clothing and equipment for wear in the field. Issue uniforms were worn unaltered by officers (except of course for badges of rank) or modified to suit individual taste. The most common alterations were to the general fit and the collar, the latter often replaced by a smarter one. But clothing stores and unit stocks were also subject to restrictions and non-delivery due to over-extended lines of supply, and it became increasingly difficult to supply other ranks besides officers. In August 1943, both the army and Waffen-SS took steps to improve the situation by arranging for better quality second-hand or tailor-made articles to be collected and resold to self-providers at three times the listed price of an issue item, [6] and in exchange for a uniform voucher (Uniform-Bezugschein).

**Notes :**

1. Handbuch für den SS-Führer des Verwaltungsdienstes der Waffen-SS., 1943., D II a) Bekleidungswesen im Kriege b) Kleiderkasse., pp. 1–3.
2. See for example V.Bl.d.W.-SS., Nr.11, 1 June 1942, Ziff.182. Beihilfe für die Uniformänderung der Polizei-Offiziere bei Übernahme zur
3. Waffen-SS.
   Handbuch für den SS-Führer des Verwaltungsdienstes der Waffen-SS.
4. Ibid.
5. Ibid.
6. V.Bl.d.W.-SS., Nr.16, 15 August 1943, Ziff.298.

**Replacement**
### 428. Care and replacement of clothing.[1]
In view of the supply situation on the textile and leather market it is the duty of every commander to make his officers and men appreciate the need to take the utmost care of equipment.

Those guilty of careless or negligent loss shall, besides being punished, replace in full the articles that they have lost.

Every unnecessary loss of clothing and equipment must be severely, punished by commanders.

I have ordered that, as in army, replacement units will in future be equipped with only lace-up ankle boots and gaiters ; Marching boots (Knobelbecher) will now only be available to soldiers of the field army.

The corresponding orders will be issued by the chief of the Verwaltungsamt-SS.

There is no end of complaints from Straubing Prison (Collecting point for old material) concerning the deliberate and senseless damage to articles of service clothing.

I have instructed the Chief of the Verwaltungsamt-SS to make in future the guilty persons pay for any damage caused, in addition to any punishment imposed.

Moreover, I shall make the allocation of replacement clothing dependent on the condition of the old articles of clothing surrendered.

In the interests of the adequate equipment of the Waffen-SS I expect all officers to appreciate fully the supply situation and to act accordingly.

Jüttner
SS-Gruppenführer und
Generalleutnant der Waffen-SS

In order to maintain a good appearance and not prejudice the reputation of the Waffen-SS, soldiers on leave or detached from units in the field, were to exchange their bad uniforms for better ones at their nearest SS Garrison Headquarters (SS-Standortkommandantur).[2]

From 15 June until 15 July 1943 the SS Garrison Headquarters in Berlin and Vienna were responsible for replacing the bad clothing of SS soldiers arriving from the eastern front.[3]

**Notes :**

1. V.Bl.d.W.-SS, Nr.20, 1 November 1941, Ziff. 428.
2. Ibid Nr.3, 1 February 1942, Ziff.43.
3. Ibid Nr.12, 15 June 1943, Ziff.218.

## Return and disposal

On completion of his term of service every Waffen-SS soldier was instructed to return to his unit all articles of clothing and equipment with which he had been issued. There were obviously many cases of soldiers acting dishonestly and from September 1940 soldiers were not released until everything had been handed in. Needy soldiers without the means to purchase a set of civilian clothing could apply for one at the Winter Welfare Service competent at their place of discharge.[1]

Once used clothing had been handed in it was sorted and those articles still suitable for further use were retained intact. Worn out clothing was dismantled and the cloth used for repairing other uniforms or as rags.

### 120. Old material.[2]

Further to various inquiries it is again pointed out that requirements of repair materials (patches, buttons, badges and rags etc.) have to be covered as far as possible by taking them from old articles of clothing. As evidence of the removal of repair materials one shall surrender — in the case of blouses, greatcoats and shirts — the collar and band, and — in the case of trousers and underpants — the waistband, together with the rest of the old material.

V 3/031/2.41.

### 121. Earth-grey clothing.[3]

As from the 1 April 1941 earth-grey clothing will be issued as working clothing in civilian work camps. From this date onwards, therefore, the wearing of earth-grey clothing in the Waffen-SS is forbidden. All articles of earth-grey clothing (tunics, trousers, greatcoats, field caps, surcoats, drill uniforms and ski clothing) still in the possession of units are to be surrendered at once to Straubing Prison Old Material Utilisation Office (Altmaterial-Verwertungsstelle). One shall remove all insignia from the articles to be surrendered for use on the field-grey training (Exerziergarnitur) clothing. Notification of the surrender of the above clothing is to be given by means of a list of the articles surrendered, to the Verwaltungsamt-SS by the 31 March 1941.

In the case of need an application may be made for the replacement of earth-grey by field-grey clothing.

V 3/341/2.41.

As from October 1943 all old clothing belonging to units in the Reich, Czechoslovakia, the General Government and occupied Western Europe was collected and sent quarterly to the Administrative Section of Straubing Prison. All articles collected on the eastern front were sent (depending on the availability of empty transport) to clothing depots at:[4]

Oulu (Finnland)
Riga (Nordabschnitt)
Bobruisk (Mittelabschnitt)
Dnjepropetrowsk (Südabschnitt)
Betscherek (Südost)

Old clothing was issued to concentration camp inmates or foreign workers, or pulped down for re-working. Metal articles were dismantled, the metals separated and used by the armament industry. As the raw material situation worsened the importance of this scrap was not underestimated.

## KOPFBEDECKUNG
Head-dress
### Feldmütze (Schiffchen) a.A.
Field cap (boat-shaped) old pattern

With the introduction of the field-grey field service uniform in 1937, the earth-grey field cap (Vol. 3, p. 38) was also manufactured in field-grey material.* Insignia remained the same, and consisted of a white metal death's head button in front (later painted field-grey), and the SS national emblem machine-embroidered in white silk on a black triangular ground on the left side of the flap. In 1939 an inverted chevron (Soutache) in Waffenfarbe was authorised for wear on the front of the cap, above the button, army style. This practice was officially discontinued in July 1942.

### Feldmütze fur Unterführer
N.C.O.'s field cap

Continuing a practice borrowed from the army, N.C.O.'s in the SS-VT wore their service caps on all occasions when a steel helmet was not specified. In 1938, this practice was recognised by the introduction of a special N.C.O.'s peaked field cap.

* The black version for wear with the black service uniform was retained for personnel in armoured units.

## Notes:
1. SS-Befehls-Blatt., Nr.8, 5 September 1940, Ziff.25.
2. V.Bl.d.W.-SS., Nr.4, 1 March 1940, Ziff.120.
3. Ibid. Ziff.121.
4. Ibid. Nr.16, 15 August 1943, Ziff.298.

## Ziff.15: Subject. SS field-grey field cap for N.C.O.'s.[1]

It has been ordered that the SS field cap, without chin strap or wire stiffener (Mützendraht), is to be worn. It must be borne in mind, that it is not to be worn as a service cap, but as a field cap, and this fact has been taken into account when designing the cap. All caps currently in use must have the chin strap and stiffener removed.

Although initially introduced as an N.C.O.'s cap, it continued to be worn well on into the war by N.C.O.'s and officers (many of whom were former N.C.O.s) in the field. The cap had a field-grey top, and soft field-grey cloth covered peak, black band, and white piping. Badges were originally in white metal, but either metal, machine-embroidered (from Panzer beret) or woven patterns were used. The December 1939 order laid down that in the vicinity of the barracks, senior N.C.O.s (Portepée-Unterführer) could wear the field-grey service cap with field-grey uniform. On all other occasions, when a steel helmet was not specified, the other ranks' field cap (Schiffchen) should be worn. However, amendments to the order permitted the wearing out of the old pattern N.C.O.'s field cap.[2]

## Dienstmütze

Service cap

Officers were the first to receive an earth-grey peaked service cap in 1935, and by 1937 it was being manufactured with a field-grey top. It was worn by commissioned ranks** on duty, on all occasions when a steel helmet was not specified. After the introduction of an officer's field cap in 1939, the peaked cap was worn with service dress, and, after the outbreak of war, with walking-out dress.

Officers' caps were made of field-grey cloth, with black velvet band and white piping for all officers up to and including SS-Staf. Senior officers with the rank of SS-Oberführer and above and aluminium piping. The peak was made of lacquered black fibre (Vulkanfiber), although softer lacquered leather peaks were also worn, albeit unofficially. Chin cords were made of two twisted aluminium cords, and were fastened to the cap with two 13 mm white metal buttons. Badges on the field-grey peaked cap were supposed to have been in aluminium finish, but silver plated ones were also worn, as

** The officers cap was also worn by graduate officer cadets (SS-Stand. Ob.Ju.) awaiting promotion to SS-Ustuf., and by SS-Hauptscharführer d.Res. in the medical or vetrinary services.[5] For the various regulations governing the wearing of coloured piping on the peaked cap, see the section dealing with Waffenfarben.

Top to bottom: Old pattern field cap for other ranks and N.C.O.'s field cap with cloth peak.

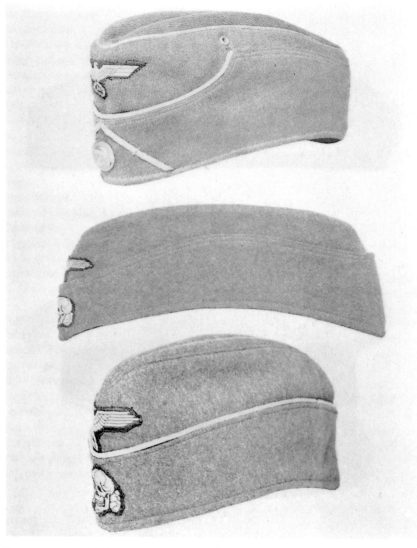

Top to bottom: 1938 model army officers field cap converted for SS use. New pattern field cap for other ranks. 1940 model Waffen-SS officers field cap.

were woven or embroidered badges. In June 1940, wearing of the white topped summer peaked cap by Waffen-SS officers was forbidden.[3]

The other ranks' version of the cap was first introduced in 1939, for wear by senior N.C.O.s in the vicinity of the barracks, and it was only after the black uniform had ceased to be worn as a walking-out dress that other ranks were issued with, or allowed to purchase, the field-grey peaked cap for wear when walking out. It had a field-grey trikot top, black cloth band, and white piping. The chin strap was black leather, and the peak was black fibre. Badges were white or matt-grey metal.

Contrary to regulations obsolete patterns of SS cap badges were worn on both officers' and other ranks' service caps. During the war the difficulty in obtaining SS insignia meant that national emblems of the army and other political organisations were worn instead of the regulation SS pattern. Initially, manufacture and retailing of field-grey SS peaked caps was controlled by the RZM, but in February 1941 they were freed from RZM control, and from then on were obtainable from private hatters and uniform outfitters, although the insignia was still only obtainable from the RZM, or one of its outlets.[4] As a result of the difficulty of obtaining SS caps and insignia, many officers purchased army caps, had a black velvet band fitted over the dark green one, and wore the national emblems of the army (or other political organisations) instead of the regulation emblem. (See, for example, the illustration on p. 91.)

The following unusual and unofficial practices regarding wearing of the service cap have been noted:

1. Wearing of the cap without chin cords or strap.
2. A photograph shows an officer in Russia wearing what appears to be a field-grey cloth cover over his service cap.

### Feldmütze (Schiffchen) für Führer

Officer's field cap (boat-shaped)

The December 1939 order required that officers obtain the new field cap (boat-shaped in the air-force cut) by 1 January 1940.[6] Prior to this date there had not been a regulation officer's field cap. Many officers had unofficially purchased the 1938 model army officer's field cap, in black or field-grey, and replaced or covered the national cockade with either the metal SS death's head, or the small white metal one from the army Panzer troops collar patch. There is at least one recorded instance of an SS officer wearing the army field cap with army insignia with Waffen-SS uniform.[7]

The 1939-model officer's field cap was made of field-grey trikot with aluminium piping around the top of the flap. In November 1940, however, Himmler amended his earlier order, and restricted the wearing of aluminium piping to senior officers with the rank of SS-Oberführer and above. All other officers were to wear white piping. This order may have been rescinded, but in any case nobody appears to have taken any notice of it. [8]

Insignia on an officer's field cap consisted of the national emblem and death's head, both of which were worn in front. They were machine woven in aluminium thread on a black ground. A Soutache in Waffenfarbe was also to be worn in front. According to regulations the correct distance between the ends of the Soutache was 9 cm.

### Feldmütze (Schiffchen) n.A.
Field cap (boat-shaped) new pattern

In November 1940 a new style field-grey cloth (black for Panzer troops) field cap in the air-force cut was introduced. [9] Insignia on caps for other ranks was basically the same as for officers, but woven in a silver grey (later matt-grey) artificial silk thread. At first the Soutache in Waffenfarbe was sewn to the front of the flap of the cap, but in order to facilitate the changing of the Soutache and cut down on make-up time, it was decided to pass the Soutache through a loop at its apex and sew it at both ends only. [10] Wearing the Soutache was discontinued in September 1942. [11]

### Einheitsfeldmütze Modell 1943
Standard field cap, Model 1943

By 1943 practical experience at the front had shown the boat-shaped field cap to be impractical, as it afforded insufficient shading from the glare of the sun, and insufficient protection to the ears and back of the neck in cold weather. Since it could be worn in many different ways it also tended to destroy the uniform appearance of a unit. The mountain cap, which had been issued in limited numbers before the war for training in mountainous regions, was smart, practical* and popular.

### 355. Field cap. [12]
Instead of the existing field cap[s] (boat-shaped), a new field cap in the same cut and manufacture as the mountain cap is to be introduced on practical grounds. The field cap is black for Panzer troops, and field-grey for all other units. Designation and article number remains unchanged. The field cap[s] (boat-shaped) may be worn out.

SS-FHA/Ia

* It was impractical in the sense that crews of enclosed armoured vehicles were permitted to wear it back to front, since the large peak made it difficult to use optical equipment.

Top to bottom: 1943 model field cap for other ranks and officers. 1943 model field cap of late manufacture with final pattern cap badge.

Top to bottom: Peaked service cap for senior officers, officers and other ranks.

The issue standard field cap was made of field-grey cloth,** and was similar in cut to the mountain cap, with large cloth covered peak and flap that fastened in front, with at first two and then one button, which could be lowered to cover ears, side and back of the head, and chin. Officers had aluminium piping around the crown of the cap.

At first the same insignia was worn as on the new pattern field cap. The death's head was worn in front, and the national emblem on the left side of the flap. In order to save time the width of the flap in front was slightly reduced, and both badges worn in front. Since it was quicker and easier to sew *one* badge, a new pattern, incorporating the national emblem *and* the death's head on a triangular base was introduced later in 1943. The new insignia was produced in two patterns. The first was machine-embroidered in matt-grey and black artificial silk on a triangular field-grey or black (for the black cap) cloth ground. The second pattern was machine-woven in a continuous strip, although the design remained basically similar. There was no officer's version of this insignia. Although primarily designed for the M.1943 cap, this insignia also appeared on other patterns of field cap, which remained in service until the end of the war.

The following unofficial practices regarding wearing the standard field cap have been noted:

1. Wearing of metal cap insignia in place of the woven pattern.
2. Wearing of a combination of woven and cloth insignia.
3. Wearing of the army M.43 field cap complete with army insignia, but the national cockade either replaced or covered by a metal or woven death's head.
4. Wearing of M.43 caps made of white material with winter clothing.
5. Wearing of M.43 caps made of light coloured lightweight materials.
6. Wearing of M.43 caps with the flaps covered with fur.
7. Wearing of ski caps of civilian manufacture either with or without SS insignia.

**Stahlhelm**

Steel helmet

Initially the SS-VT had been issued with a modified version of the 1916 model steel helmet, or SS/RZM model. (See Vol. 3, pp. 39 – 41.) On 1 November 1935 the chief of the SS-Hauptamt, notified all units of the SS-VT that since deliveries of the field-grey Wehrmacht helmet from the Reich War Ministry were expected before the end of the year, the introduction of the grey-green canvas cover for the black one was no longer necessary. The black helmet in the possession of the SS-VT was to be used for parades.[13] This notice does not specify which model helmet was to be delivered, but most probably it was the Reichswehr model, which was, at the time, being replaced by the 1935 model in the armed forces.

The smaller 1935 model steel helmet was first issued to the SS-VT in 1936, and by the beginning of the war had been issued in both field-grey and black finishes. The obsolete 1916 model and RZM helmets continued in use with security and Ersatz units until withdrawn in March 1941.[14] The 1935 model was made in five basic sizes, weighing from 681-1,200 grms. The lining was of natural coloured leather (perforated for ventilation) which could be adjusted to fit the head by means of a drawstring and was attached to and suspended from an aluminium band fixed to the shell of the helmet by three cotter-pins. The two-piece black leather chin strap was fastened on both sides to rings on the band, and buckled on the left side by a single pronged white metal buckle. In 1943, both cost factor and production speed were improved when the helmet was modified with an uncrimped brim.

## Finish

Before the war the steel helmet had a smooth surface with a semi-matt field-grey finish. It was forbidden to alter this finish either by polishing or greasing. In March 1940 it was decided, for camouflage reasons, to apply a new slightly rough finish (schiefergrau). Until supplies of this new paint were made available helmets were to be camouflaged temporarily with earth or clay. During the war many different finishes were applied; although too varied and numerous to list fully, mention must be made of the use of common whitewash when 'the field' was a snow covered landscape!

## Wappenschilde

Escutcheons

From September 1935 the standard escutcheons of the SS were worn on the steel helmet (Vol. 3, p. 41). These were normally applied by transfer, although some were hand painted. In March 1940, it was decided, for camouflage reasons, to omit or remove the national escutcheon, which was worn on the left side of the helmet. In November 1943, the SS runes, worn on the right side, was also discontinued, although it continued to appear until the end of the war.[15]

## Accessories

The question of camouflaging steel helmets was never as important in the Waffen-SS, as it was in the army, since the Waffen-SS had been issued with a camouflage cover as early as 1938. (See section on camouflage clothing.) In addition to the cover, Waffen-SS personnel used various types

Top to bottom: 1935 model steel helmet with semi-matt field-grey finish and national colours. 1935 model with matt rough finish. 1st pattern steel helmet cover.

Members of SS Death's Head Infantry Regiment 2 during winter training at Münsingen manouvre ground, winter 1939-40. They wear the first pattern field-grey greatcoat with collar piping and have painted their helmets with whitewash.

of adjustable straps fitted to the helmet so that foliage and other camouflage materials could be held in place.[16] Camouflage netting in string or wire was also used.

## Notes:

1. SS-Befehls-Blatt., Nr.2, 25 February 1939, Ziff.15.
2. See Appendix I.
3. V.Bl.d.W.-SS., Nr.2, 15 June 1940, Ziff.46.
4. Mitteilungsblatt der RZM. Nr.2, 25 January 1941. p. 10.
5. V.Bl.d.W.-SS., Nr.23, 15 December 1941, Ziff.487.
6. See Appendix I.
7. Bender/Taylor, Vol. 1, p. 85 with illustration.
8. Der Reichsführer-SS, SS-Befehl (Abschrift), Betr.: Feldgraue Uniform der Waffen-SS, Sicherheitspolizei und des SD, Bezug Mein Befehl vom 10 May 1940, Berlin, den 5 November 1940.
9. V.Bl.d.W.-SS., Nr.21, 1 November 1940, Ziff.
10. Ibid., Nr.20, 15 October 1940, Ziff. 269.
11. Ibid., Nr.17, 1 September 1942, Ziff.309.
12. Ibid., Nr.19, 1 October 1943, Ziff.355.
13. Der Chef des SS-Hauptamtes. I/U 1 Nr.014481/35 Betr.: Überzug für Stahlhelme. Berlin den 1 November 1935.
14. V.Bl.d.W.-SS., Nr.6, 1 April 1941, Ziff.159.
15. Ibid., Nr.21, 1 November 1943, Ziff.402.
16. See page 113.

# BEKLEIDUNG
## Clothing
### Feldbluse
#### Field blouse

In 1937 a new field-grey field blouse and long grey trousers began to replace the old earth-grey service uniform. The new field blouse was based on the 1935 army model but retained certain SS features, such as the collar, which was the same colour as the blouse, designed to be worn primarily open but easily closed. It had slanting slash side pockets with buttoned flap instead of the pleated army patch pockets. The collar (and collar patches and some patterns of shoulder strap) was piped in black and aluminium twisted cord until August 1940 when it was discontinued.[1]

Formation of the SS-Totenkopf and SS-Polizei divisions at the close of 1939 necessitated the supply, by the army, of sufficient quantities of army field uniforms to equip them.[2] The December 1939 order described the field blouse as being of army cut with dark green collar, button-on collar liner, and patch pockets. The blouse was to be worn open with brown shirt and black tie. When training, on manoeuvres, or on special occasions it could be worn closed by order of the commander. Amendments to this order stated that the old-style SS blouse (with the same colour collar) was to be worn out; and that alterations to the field blouse were forbidden.[2] If the war continued for any length of time, the field blouse would again be supplied with the same colour collar. The amendment went on to state that the blouse was to be worn closed at the neck, and only opened by order. The May 1940 order described the field blouse as being basically the same for officers and men, and that in principle it was to be worn open with shirt and tie and only closed by special order.[3]

The results of these contradictory orders can be clearly seen in any Waffen-SS group photo, where some of the men are wearing the blouse with the collar open at the neck, whilst others wear it closed. It was just this sort of lack of uniformity that Himmler was trying to prevent.

By the time of the campaigns in France and the Low Countries, personnel of the SS-Verfügungs-Truppe-Division were mostly still wearing the SS field blouse, with just a few army patterns beginning to appear. The bulk of the SS-Totenkopf and SS-Polizei divisions on the other hand, were equipped with army field uniforms. In 1940, the field blouse collar began, as predicted in the December 1939 order, to be made of the same material as the rest of the blouse, instead of dark green. The next modifications to the field blouse took place step by step throughout the war, for the purpose of economising on material and labour. From 1942 patch pockets were made without pleats,

One of a series of photographs entitled 'a day in the life of the Leibstandarte SS Adolf Hitler' 22 November 1938, showing a soldier learning firing positions under the watchful eye of an SS-Unterscharführer who wears typical everyday dress consisting of an army tunic, obsolete earth-grey breeches, and the M38 N.C.O.'s field cap with chin strap.

Typical training uniform being worn by Leibstandarte SS Adolf Hitler recruits on 22 November 1938. The helmet is the old black 1916 model, and the army field blouse is being worn with the first pattern national emblem and no cuff-band. The tapered trousers (Stiefelhose) and high boots are in the process of being worn out.

and later the lower edge of the flaps was straightened. Since wartime materials had less tensile strength than in peace time, it was necessary to increase the five front buttons to six. Other modifications and simplifications were made to the lining and manufacture of the field blouse, but none of them altered its outward appearance.

After extensive field trials with army units, a new field uniform (Felduniform 1944) began to appear in late 1944, but never in sufficient numbers to radically alter the appearance of the Waffen-SS. [4] The new field blouse bore certain similarities to the British battledress, and consisted of a short blouse with wide waistband and patch pockets, and long tapering trousers which were designed to be worn either inside the gaiter or marching boot. The uniform required considerably less cloth than the earlier models, and was specially designed to facilitate rapid manufacture by semi-skilled labour; the M.1944 field blouse insignia was unchanged. The colour of the uniform was also changed from field-grey to Feldgrau 44 (the official designation for the new grey-brown colour). Existing stocks of field-grey and foreign materials were made-up into the new field uniform, thus many different shades of field-grey emerged.

**Seitenhaken**

Belt hooks

Each field blouse was usually issued with four field-grey painted steel or aluminium hooks of special design. These hooks were attached to a fabric strap which formed part of the blouse lining. The strap was designed to take the weight of a fully loaded waist belt supported by a metal hook.

**Feldhose**

Field trousers

The 1937 model SS field trousers were identical to the 1935 army model. Both had long straight legs, two side pockets and a watch pocket in front. They could be adjusted at the waist by means of a buckled strap and were designed to be worn with braces.

At first trousers were manufactured in new-grey cloth, but from 1939 onwards they were to match the blouse in field-grey. [6] In July 1942 new standard trousers (Keilhose) were introduced. [7]

### 220. Introduction of new items of clothing.

For the Waffen-SS a new standard lace-up ankle boot, and field-grey Keilhose, will replace the old marching boot and long cloth trousers. With the Keilhose, cloth gaiters or puttees (in the summer) or canvas gaiters (in winter) will be worn. Motor-cyclists and official pillion passengers (but not sidecar passengers) N.C.O.s and men in engineer units and guard battalions, will retain marching boots.

Kdo.d.W.-SS/Ia

In September 1943 an attempt was made to standardise the various different types of trousers and breeches in use in the Waffen-SS.

### 357. Introduction of new and alteration of existing clothing. [7]

For the rest of the war the following are introduced or altered:

1. Riding breeches in drill with cloth belt, side and hip pockets with buttons, fob pocket with flap, and four loops at the waist for the belt.
   Designation and article number:
   Riding breeches, drill. Article No. B/173.

2. Instead of the existing riding breeches, breeches will be manufactured as 1 above.
   Designation and article number:
   Riding breeches, grey. Article No. B/54.

3. Instead of the existing drill trousers, a drill trousers with cloth belt, button fastening at ankle, pockets, and loops are 1 above will be introduced.
   Designation and article number:
   Drill trousers, undyed or rush green . . . Article No. B/171.

4. The expected issue of cloth trousers (Keilschnitt)* to replace the long trousers and ski trousers remains unchanged. Trousers described in 1 and 4 above may be worn with or without braces.
   New trousers will be issued in relation to production.
   Existing patterns may be worn out.

New trousers (Feldhose 44) were introduced with the new Field Uniform 44. They had a built-in cloth belt, side, fob and two hip pockets (one was intended for a field dressing pack) all with buttoned flaps. The bottom of the trouser leg had a drawstring so that it could be fastened tightly around the ankle for wear with gaiters or puttees. [8]

   * The trousers with a built-in cloth belt were introduced because the wearing of braces was impractical in the field and impossible with shirt-sleeve order. The new trousers were known also as Rundbundhose.

### Notes:

1. V.Bl.d.W.-SS., Nr.5, 3 August 1940, Ziff.
2. Soldaten wie andere auch, pp. 268 and 274.
3. See Appendix I.
4. Die Deutsche Wehrmacht 1934-bis 1945, Heft 1 with illustration.
5. See Appendix I.
6. V.bl.d.W.-SS., Nr.13, 1 July 1942, Ziff. 220.
7. Ibid., Nr.19, 1 October 1943, Ziff. 357.
8. Die Deutsche Wehrmacht 1934-bis 1945, Heft 33 with illustration.

Members of SS Regiment Deutschland wearing the M1937 field blouse France 1940. They have removed their collar patches to avoid positive identification of their unit by the enemy.

A group of N.C.O.s from the 14th Company SS-Pz. Gren. Rgt. 38 (17.SS-Pz. Gren. Div. Götz von Berlichingen) wearing typical service dress with various patterns of field blouse and footwear then in use, France 1944.

This photograph of two young SS men captured by the Americans during the battle of Bastogne shows the general shoddiness and state of deterioration of uniform at the end of the war.

German prisoners rounded up by the U.S. Seventh Army are confronted by freed inmates of Dachau concentration camp, April 1944. The SS mountain trooper wears the SS version of the edelweiss on his standard field cap, and the short M44 field blouse.

An SS-Oberscharführer wearing a privately purchased officers' quality service dress for walking-out.

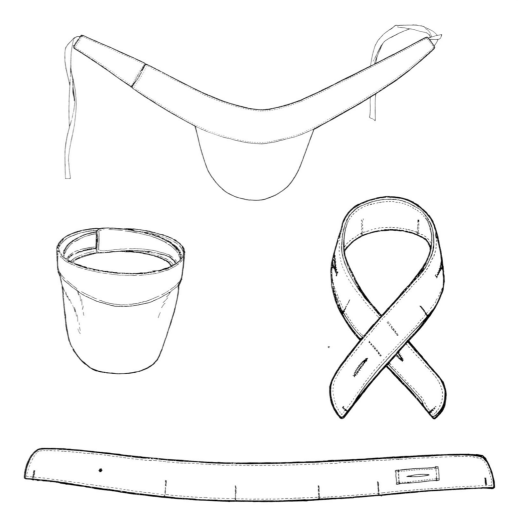

Neckcloth and collar liner.

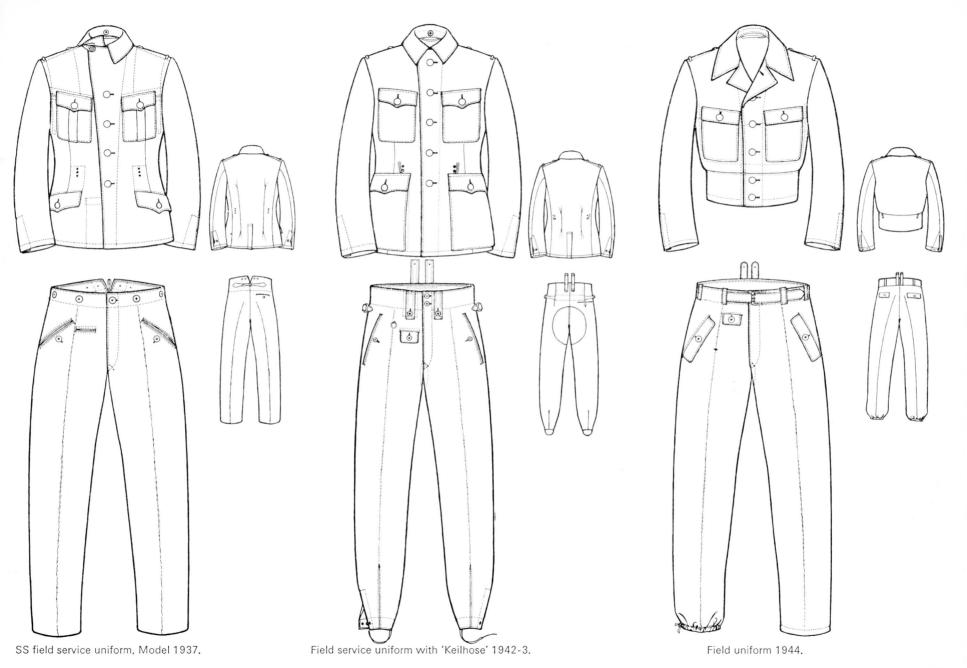

SS field service uniform, Model 1937.

Field service uniform with 'Keilhose' 1942-3.

Field uniform 1944.

23

SS-Ostubaf Klingenberg wearing an unusual version of the pre-war tunic with closed collar. Another photograph of the same officer shows the tunic with side patch pockets and buttoned flaps and pleats.

## Rock
Tunic

Until 1939, officers in the SS-Verfügungstruppe had only one field-grey tunic (Rock), which was made of field-grey trikot, and was identical in cut to the black SS service tunic. It was worn on all occasions with a brown shirt and black tie. After the general introduction of the field blouse, officers were permitted to continue wearing the tunic on all occasions when it was convenient to do so, such as in the office or off duty. The commander specified which should be worn so that the officers' corps was uniformly dressed.[1] The tunic was also made of lightweight field-grey gabardine or moleskin with matching breeches for wear during summer.[2]

At the beginning of the war, the more impecunious SS officers avoided the expense of having to buy an extra army field blouse by having their tunics converted into field blouses by the addition of a dark bluish-green stand-and-fall collar.[3] Others had tailored alterations so that the collar could be worn closed at the neck. Some, however, had tunics specially made with dark green collars, although this was expressly forbidden.[4] Waffen-SS officers continued to wear their tunics, in regulation cut or with the above modifications, as an undress or walking-out uniform throughout the war.

## Weisser Sommerrock
White summer tunic

On 27 June 1939, Himmler authorised the wearing of a white summer tunic by SS officers between 1 April and 30 September.[5] It could be worn as an undress uniform with long black (occasionally white) trousers and either black or white topped peaked cap. On 15 June 1940, and for the duration of the war, the authorisation was withdrawn,[6] but it is almost certain that the comparatively few officers equipped with the white tunic had it dyed field-grey, and continued to wear it during the war.

A number of officers continued to wear lightweight field blouses in various kinds of washable white materials. The cut and insignia worn on these unofficial extra blouses varied considerably.[7]

Another type of washable white jacket was worn by orderlies (Ordonnanzen) while serving at table.

## Notes:

1. See Appendix I.
2. Original example in gabardine in the author's collection.
3. Original example in author's collection.
4. See Bender/Taylor, Vol. 1, p. 41 with illustration.
5. Der Reichsführer-SS. Betr: Weisser Sommerrock, Berlin, 27 June 1939.
6. V.Bl.D.W.-SS., Nr.2, 15 June 1940, Ziff.46.
7. See Bender/Taylor, Vol. 1, pp. 42 & 76, with illustrations.

## Feldbluse (Führer)
(Field blouse (officers))

The Reichswehr pattern officer's field blouse had been adopted by at least one officer in the Leibstandarte Adolf Hitler as early as 1935, but it was not until 1939 that officers throughout the armed SS began equipping themselves with a field-grey field blouse for wear on active duty. During this transitional period, a number of stop-gap measures were taken by officers, who either modified their tunics, or obtained an issue field blouse from stores.

The December 1939 order, concerning the field-grey uniform of the Waffen-SS, stipulated that an officer's blouse was to be identical in cut to that of the men (i.e. the issue blouse), and worn open at the neck with brown shirt and black tie; it could be worn closed only if men had been ordered to close theirs. Wearing the dark bluish-green stand-and-fall collar (army officer's field blouse collar) was forbidden.[1] This is interesting, because it shows Himmler's latent dislike of the stiff-necked Prussian junker look, which he did not want emulated by his ''classless' SS. This order had no sooner been typed out when it was amended by the SS-Hauptamt. In future, wearing the blouse open with shirt and tie was to be discontinued for the duration of the war. It was now to be worn closed, opened only by special order, as in the army.[2] Waffen-SS officers now began to order army field blouses, but Himmler insisted that the stand-and-fall collar was to be fastened with one hook, not two![3]

But on 10 May 1940, Himmler amended his December 1939 field blouse order, stipulating once again (and contradicting the previous amendment) that the field blouse for officers and men was to be identical in all respects, and in principle was to be worn open with shirt and tie. Only on special occasions (rain, storm, or cold etc.) could the blouse be closed over shirt and tie. The order went on to say that the blouse be altered to close lightly and comfortably over the tie.[4] Few officers had either time or inclination to observe such subtilies.

Throughout the war, then, Waffen-SS officers, wore either a privately tailored field blouse in army officer's cut, or with slight differences, such as slanting slash side pockets with buttoned flaps, as on the SS tunic, or with a stand-and-fall collar made of the same material as the blouse. During the course of the war the buttons on the front of some tailor-made blouses were reduced from six to five. In action officers tended to wear the issue field blouse. Field blouses for summer wear were also made of lightweight gabardine, moleskin, or drill in various shades of grey or field-grey. Captured Soviet groundsheets were in plentiful supply on the eastern front, and the olive green waterproof cotton duck was often made up into lightweight field blouses.

SS-Ogruf. 'Sepp' Dietrich and members of his staff near Charkov in April 1943. L-R, SS-Hstuf. Möbius wearing issue uniform with officer's badge of rank. Dietrich for once wearing a reasonably regulation officer's service dress. SS-Stubaf, and Divisional Operations Officer (1a) Lehrmann in regulation officer's field service uniform, and SS-Stubaf. Meyer in a pre-war tunic which has been converted into a field blouse by the addition of a stand-and-fall collar and still retains the early form of national emblem.

An unidentified SS-Obersturmführer from the SS Death's Head Division, photographed sometime after June 1942, wearing a tailor-made lightweight field blouse for summer wear.

## Insignia

Generally speaking all insignia could be worn on both tunic and field blouse. On the tunic and tailor-made field blouse, insignia tended to be of officer quality. Collar patch emblems, national emblem, and cuff-band inscription were usually hand-embroidered. In fact, the May 1940 order actually goes so far as to stipulate that only on the tunic were hand-embroidered trade badges to be worn. On the field blouse, officers were to wear the machine-embroidered pattern. In 1940, officers' insignia began to be machine woven in aluminium thread, and by the end of the war it had mostly replaced the hand-embroidered pattern on most officers' uniforms.

Officers usually wore the field blouse with insignia as issued. Since bright aluminium embroidery was dangerously conspicuous in action officers retained the issue insignia only adding their rank badges, often omitting the twisted aluminium cord from the collar patches.

## Stiefelhose (Breeches) und lange Hose

Breeches and long trousers

The officer's tunic was worn with tailor-made new-grey (neugrau) trikot breeches without piping. Riding breeches were made of a special heavy new-grey trikot, and were usually reinforced with grey buckskin on the seat and inside leg, or just at the knee.[1] With the lightweight summer tunic, breeches were made of matching field-grey gabardine or moleskin.

Off-duty officers could wear long new-grey trousers with white piping irrespective of branch of service.[2] Piping in Waffenfarbe was introduced but discontinued after 31 December 1940.[3] Both breeches and trousers had similar pocket fittings — two slanting slash pockets fastened with a button, a watch pocket in front, and a straight slash pocket with button on the left hip. Trousers were fitted with either leather or elastic footstraps (Stege). Trousers and breeches described above continued to be worn with the tunic and field blouse throughout the war, but front-line officers tended to wear long field-grey issue trousers, or cavalry breeches with the field blouse of other ranks. In August 1944 officers were ordered to wear long trousers with corresponding footwear (when their men had been ordered to turn out in long trousers without gaiters). They were also to wear long trousers (instead of breeches and boots) with informal service dress (Kleiner Dienstanzug) and reporting dress (Meldeanzug).

## Notes:

1. SS-Kleiderkasse Katalog., pp. 5, 18, 25 with illustration.
2. See Appendix II.
3. Der Reichsführer-SS., SS-Befehl; Betrifft: Feldgraue Uniform der Waffen-SS, Sicherheitspolizei und des SD., Berlin, den 5 November 1940.

SS medical officers who volunteered for medical duties at the liberated concentration camp at Neuengamme, May 1945. The SS-Ustuf. on the left wears the 1944 model field uniform. The officer in the centre (whose badges of rank on the collar patch and shoulder straps do not match) wears the 1943 model field blouse, trousers and marching boots. The SS-Ostuf. on the right wears standard field cap, tailor-made field blouse from issue quality cloth, and officer's breeches and boots.

27

SS-Ostuf. Böhmer wearing other ranks uniform congratulates members of his battalion. The SS-Stabsscharführer (Spiess) wears a most unusual winter head-dress, while the rest of the men wear both patterns of the field cap, and greatcoats with either the dark green or field-grey collar.

## Mantel
### Greatcoat

The original earth-grey greatcoat was identical in cut to the black one, and had an earth-grey collar which was piped in black and aluminium twisted cord until August 1940. Shoulder straps and collar patches were always worn, but not the national emblem.

Introduction of the field-grey uniform was accompanied by a matching regulation army greatcoat with dark bluish-green collar. This is confirmed by the December 1939 dress regulations which stated that the Waffen-SS greatcoat was to retain its existing cut but have a dark green collar.[1] Both the SS and army pattern greatcoats were worn side by side, with or without collar cord and patches, until the old earth-grey model was recalled in March 1941.[2] For the rest of the war, and until the introduction of the standard greatcoat, the Waffen-SS wore the army pattern greatcoat which at first had a dark green and later a field-grey collar.

### 28. Standard greatcoat.[3]

In order to continue the standardisation of the uniforms of the armed forces, a standard greatcoat is hereby introduced.

Designation and article number:

Cloth greatcoat . . . Article No. B/87.

The old surcoat (Übermantel) for drivers, and the old pattern cloth greatcoat will continue to be worn. Existing stocks will be used up.

SS-FHA/Ia

## Führermantel
### Officer's greatcoat

By July 1935, the Leibstandarte Adolf Hitler had been issued with earth-grey uniforms, which included an earth-grey greatcoat with matching collar. While certain officers drew issue greatcoat from regimental stocks, others wore privately tailored army patterns, with collar of slightly darker face cloth (Abzeichentuch). Both issue and privately made greatcoats had collar patches, shoulder straps, and cuff-band, but at first the national emblem appeared only on private coats. At this time the greatcoat collar was not piped in twisted cord. Following army regulations, the colour of the greatcoat collar gradually became darker, until it was a dark bluish-green.

The next step in the development of the officer's greatcoat came in 1937, with the introduction of field-grey. Once again officers wore either issue

## Notes:

1. See Appendix I.
2. V.Bl.d.W.-SS., Nr.4, 1 March 1940, Ziff.121.
3. Ibid. Nr.2. 15 January 1944, Ziff.28.

greatcoats with appropriate insignia, or had them tailor made. The tailor-made field-grey SS officer's greatcoats differed from that of the army only in its half belt. The SS design was identical to that on the black greatcoat — being 5 cm wide and buttoning at each end. The army half belt joined in the middle where it was fastened with two buttons.[1] The issue field-grey SS greatcoat was identical to the army pattern. Collar patches, shoulder straps, and cuff-band was almost invariably worn, whereas the national emblem appeared only on some coats.

With the military development of the armed SS, there was a tendency to follow army fashions in matters of dress, which led to the removal of collar patches from the greatcoat. By the outbreak of war, the situation was pretty muddled, with officers wearing field-grey greatcoats with either matching or dark green collars, either with or without collar patches, so that a number of orders had to be issued throughout the course of the war to clarify the situation. (See section on issue greatcoats.)

Senior officers with the rank of SS-Oberführer and above were allowed to wear the greatcoat with the top three buttons undone, thus exposing silver grey lapels. In February 1941, holders of the Knight's Cross of the Iron Cross or War Service Cross were also allowed to wear the top two buttons undone and to fold back the lapels so that any decoration — which was worn at the neck — was visible.[2] A comparatively common, but unofficial practice, was the wearing of twisted aluminium cord on the dark green greatcoat collar.

According to Waffen-SS regulations all insignia could be worn on the great-coat, although, for reasons already stated, there was a tendency to follow army practice, and limit the insignia to shoulder straps, national emblem, and cuff-band. In addition to the regulation cloth greatcoat, officers were allowed to wear the following extra coats:

**Regen-Wettermantel**

Raincoat

This field-grey raincoat was first introduced in 1938,[3] and could be purchased and worn by officers and senior N.C.O.s. The only insignia officially worn on this coat were shoulder straps. During the war officers often unofficially wore the motor-cyclist's coat as a raincoat.

**Ledermantel**

Leather greatcoat

The field-grey leather greatcoat was an extremely expensive extra item of clothing, which was purchased by the wearer. It was supposed to conform to regulation greatcoat cut, but many variations in colour and cut were worn. Again, shoulder straps only were officially acceptable, but some officers wore all insignia.

SS-Ogruf. u. Gen. d. W.-SS Dietrich with officers of the 12.SS-Pz. Div. Hitlerjugend, spring 1944. Dietrich wears a regulation greatcoat with silver grey lapels and dark green Collar. Most of the other officers appear to be wearing issue greatcoats, while one has added a fur collar.

Standard greatcoat.

## Tragen der Spiegel auf dem Mantelkragen

Wearing of collar patches on the greatcoat collar

The wearing of collar patches on the greatcoat was never very uniform, and the following four orders were issued in an attempt to regularise the situation.

### 231. Collar patches on the greatcoat collar. [4]

The Reichsführer-SS has ordered that collar patches will be worn on the greatcoat collar, as well as on the blouse, by all units of the Waffen-SS. Collar patches must be put on immediately. The removal of collar patches for reasons of camouflage may only be authorised by the Reichsführer-SS.

Kdo.d.W.-SS IVa

### 169. The wearing of collar patches on the greatcoat. [5]

With immediate effect, and by order of the RFSS, the wearing of collar patches on the greatcoat must cease until further notice because of shortage of raw materials.

For the sake of uniformity, this order does not only apply to the manufacture of new collar patches for greatcoats, but those already on greatcoats must be removed and used elsewhere.

Sgd. Jüttner
SS-Gruf.u.Gen.Lt. der Waffen-SS

### 37. The wearing of collar patches on the greatcoat collar. [6]

The Reichsführer-SS has ordered:

Following the published order in the V.Bl.d.W.-SS, No. 11 of 1 June 1942, concerning the wearing of collar patches on the greatcoat, it is ordered that collar patches will be worn:

1.  By the Allgemeine-SS on all greatcoats
2.  By the Waffen-SS on all greatcoats with the exception of:

    (a)  Leather greatcoat (grey)
    (b)  Raincoat (rubberised or impregnated fabric)
    (c)  Surcoat (for drivers)
    (d)  Guard coat (fur)
    (e)  Motor-cyclists coat (rubberised)
    (f)  Field greatcoat (Feldmantel)

SS-FHA./Ia

## 2. The wearing of collar patches on the greatcoat.[7]

1. Item (Ziffer) 37 of the V.Bl.d.W.-SS., No. 3 of 1 February 1943 is hereby amended.

2. On the grounds of (shortage of) raw materials collar patches and the cuff-band will not in future be worn on issue greatcoats (truppen-eigenen Mänteln).

3. Collar patches and cuff-bands may continue to be worn on all private greatcoats with the exception of:
   (a) Leather greatcoat (grey)
   (b) Raincoat (rubberised or impregnated fabric)
   (c) Surcoat (for drivers)
   (d) Motor-cyclists coat (rubberised)
   (e) Field greatcoat (Feldmantel)

4. In the Allgemeine-SS, collar patches and cuff-bands will continue to be worn on all greatcoats.

SS-FHA/Ia

To summarise, those possessing their own private greatcoats could continue wearing collar patches, but issue greatcoats were to have the collar patches removed prior to issue, and were to be worn without insignia, with the exception of shoulder straps. In this connection it is interesting to note that even the SS Guard Battalion, which was drawn from the Leibstandarte-SS "Adolf Hitler", and which carried out guard duties at the Reichs Chancellory in Berlin, wore the greatcoat without collar patches.[8]

## Notes:

1. Uniformen-Markt. Nr.4, 1940, p. 27 with illustration.
2. V.Bl.d.W.-SS., Nr.1, 15 January 1941, Ziff.5.
3. SS-Befehls-Blatt., Nr.3, March 1938, Ziff.11.
4. V.Bl.d.W.-SS., Nr.10, 1 October 1940, Ziff.231.
5. Ibid. Nr.,11, 1 June 1942, Ziff.169.
6. Ibid. Nr., 3, 1 February 1943, Ziff.37.
7. Ibid.Nr., 1, 1 January 1945, Ziff.2.
8. Hamburger Illustrierte Nr.16, 17 April 1943, pp. 4-5 with illustrations.

Regulation field-grey raincoat being worn by an officer and senior N.C.O.

Typical issue grey woollen socks and wrist warmers. From one to four rings denoted the size of the article. One ring was the smallest.

## UNTERKLEIDUNG/WÄSCHE
(Underclothing)

Issue underclothing consisted of the following items :
1. Brown shirt
2. Neckcloth or collar liner
3. Black tie
4. White undershirt
5. White underpants (long-Johns)
6. Braces
7. Pullover
8. Handkerchiefs
9. Socks
10. Footwraps

1. Brown trikot collar-attached shirt without pockets. Replaced, together with white undershirt, by the new standard shirt in 1943.
2. The neckcloth was made of earth-grey or black cotton and was fastened around the neck by a tie-string. It was designed to be worn in conjunction with the collarless white undershirt, and to give a neat appearance when worn with the closed field blouse.

    The collar liner was issued instead of the collar-attached shirt or neckcloth. It was attached to the inside of the field blouse collar by five small buttons sewn there for this purpose and enabling easy removal for washing. The liner was white on the inside (next to the neck) and field-grey or rush green on the outside. When the field blouse was worn open at the neck, the liner was buttoned so that it followed the line of the opening. Both neckcloth and liner were discontinued after the introduction of the standard collar-attached shirt.
3. The standard SS tie was of black artificial silk as worn with the black service uniform. It was only issued together with the brown shirt.
4. The standard army issue natural coloured aertex undershirt was impractical in the front-line because of its conspicuous colour and was sometimes dyed green. It, too, was replaced by the standard shirt.
5. Long-Johns (or underpants) were made of natural coloured wool or cotton, three-quarter length, and tied at the rear of the waist and at the legs with drawstrings. They did not stand up very well to the rigours of continuous marching, so in September 1941 a special lining was made available for the 'speedy and durable improvement of underpants'.
6. Field-grey elastic braces with metal fittings and leather straps were not issued after the introduction of trousers with built-in belt. Other ranks were entitled to a pair per year.

7.  Field-grey knitted woollen pullover with long sleeves and V-neck. Pullovers with turtle necks were also issued later in the war.

9.  The grey knitted woollen socks had 1-4 bands at the top. During the second half of the war there was a tendency to wear the tapered trousers (Keilhose) inside socks and roll them over the top of ankle boots. This practice was forbidden in August 1944.

10. In the Russian army footwrap cloths were, and still are, considered to be a highly important part of an infantryman's kit, and far superior to socks, but in the German army and Waffen-SS, they were only issued if socks were not available. The footwrap cloth was square and folded around the foot. Its advantages were that it didn't slip down the foot as socks tended to do, and could be re-positioned so that the sole of the foot was always wrapped in a fresh and dry part of the cloth. Cloths were easier to wash, dried quicker, and lasted longer than socks.

### Officers[11]

1.  Officers' brown shirts for wear with the tunic were made of poplin with detached collar. White shirts were never worn with the field-grey tunic.

4.  Officers' vests were made of natural coloured wool, cotton, or aertex, and usually had short sleeves. For the winter there were long-sleeved shirts with lined fronts.

5.  Underpants were also made of wool or cotton, with an elastic waist. Special re-inforced short- or long-Johns in either light or heavyweight materials were worn for riding.

The above items were recommended by the SS Officers Clothing Counter, but officers could purchase civilian underclothing if they wished. Later in the war, shirts of almost any colour could be worn under the field blouse.

Finally, in August 1943, a standard field-grey shirt was ordered to replace the various types of shirt in use. The new pattern shirt was manufactured in various materials and colours, but the most typical were field-grey trikot or aertex. Although the introductory orders clearly state that the special badges of rank were for wear on clothing without shoulder straps, some shirts were manufactured with loops for the shoulder straps, and shoulder straps were quiet commonly worn on the shirt.

### 335. Shirt with collar attached.[12]

1.  Instead of the brown trikot shirt, and white undershirts, a grey-green collar-attached shirt will be introduced.
    Designation and article number:
    Collar-attached shirt . . . Article No. B/415.
    This shirt will be supplied as and when ready. There is no point ir. making applications for preferential delivery. Other types of shirt are to be worn out.

Top : Issue collar attached brown woollen shirt.
Bottom : Issue collar attached field-grey aertex shirt.

2. Method of wearing:
   (a) When field blouse collar is closed, the shirt collar may protrude 2 cm above that of the blouse at the point where the collar fastens, otherwise 0.5 cm only should be visible.
   (b) When the blouse collar is worn undone, the shirt collar and top shirt button are to be undone, and turned down, corresponding to the opening of the field-blouse, or the shirt collar may be placed over the blouse collar.
   (c) In warm weather the shirt may be worn without a field blouse:
      (i) By the field army outside Reich borders on any duty. Off duty it may only be worn by those troops already issued with the belted trousers, in accordance with the order of the territorial commander.
      (ii) On home territory within the confines of the barracks. On duty outside the barracks, the field blouse or drill jacket, and off duty the field blouse or tunic, must be worn. The field blouse may only be worn open on Reich territory by closed formations.
      (iii) The wearing of badges of rank on the shirt are subject to the provisions according to the V.Bl.d.W.-SS.Nr.4, 15 February 1943, Ziff.63, and attached appendix.

SS-FHA/Ia

## Handbekleidung
Gloves

Other ranks were only allowed to wear field-grey knitted woollen gloves in winter. Officers and N.C.O.s were to wear grey-green suede, buckskin, artificial or real pigskin or Nappa gloves with various kinds of fastenings, usually press stud or strap, on all occasions. During the war as raw materials became scarce and gloves more difficult to obtain on the open market, regulations governing the wearing of gloves were relaxed. By the end of the war they were only obligatory for officers when reporting or on other special occasions. For winter wear they were often lined with fur, wool, or sheepskin. There were also special reinforced gloves for riding or driving.

**Notes:**
1. V.Bl.d.W.-SS., Nr.00, 15 August 1943, Ziff.335.
5. Ibid. Nr.21, 1 September 1941, Ziff.447.
6. VM.-SS., Nr.135, 1940, Nr.199.
9. V.Bl.d W.-SS., Nr.15, 1 August 1944, Ziff.433.
11. SS-Kleiderkasse, Preisliste, Gültig ab 1 November 1940.
12. V.Bl.d.W.-SS., Nr.18, 15 August 1943, Ziff.335.

## Fussbekleidung
Footwear

The standard footwear of the SS-VT consisted of two pairs of high marching boots, one of which was for everyday use and other for best wear. The high boots were worn with tapered trousers (Stiefelhose). Beginning in 1934, the LAH received, in addition to the two pairs of high boots, a pair of lace-up ankle boots, and a pair of army marching boots (Knobelbecher or dice boxes) for field service. The tapered trousers and high boots continued to be worn for training long after the introduction of marching boots and long trousers. Ankle boots were worn with long trousers in barracks.

The first wartime economy measure was the reduction in November 1939, of the height of the shaft of marching boots from 32-41 to 29-35 cm according to size. In November 1940 the following restrictions were placed on the issue of marching boots:

### 335. Equipping of unmounted replacement personnel with marching footwear.[1]

For economy reasons unmounted personnel in replacement units, except engineers, motorcycle units and motorcyclists, are to be issued soon with a short cloth gaiter to be worn with the existing lace-up ankle boot, instead of the marching boot.

The exact date of introduction will be announced later.

The required quantity of gaiters and second pair of ankle boots must first be reported to the Verwaltungsamt der Waffen-SS by 1 December 1940. Allocation will be made according to available stocks.

After allocation of the reported requirement of cloth gaiters, marching boots will only form part of the field equipment (Feldgarnitur), and will only be issued to units of the field army as well as engineers and all kinds of motorcyclist replacements.

To what extent field units will be equipped with marching footwear is not yet certain but will be notified in due course.

Riding boots will be retained by mounted personnel in all units of the field and replacement army as hitherto.

Kdo.d.W.-SS/IVa

In July 1942 standard lace-up ankle length marching boots were introduced.[2]

### 220. Introduction of new items of clothing.

For the Waffen-SS, a standard lace-up shoe has been introduced instead of the marching boot, and field-grey Keilhose instead of the long cloth trousers.

In summer, cloth gaiters or puttees, and in winter canvas gaiters will be worn with the Keilhose.

Motor-cyclists, official pillion, but not sidecar passengers, and N.C.O.s and men in engineer units and guard battalions will retain their marching boots.

Kdo.d.W.-SS/Ia

Nearly all new footwear was issued in its natural leather colour, and was then stained and polished by the recipient. In peacetime only the best pair of boots was actually polished, while field boots were just blackened and left with a dull finish. In 1944, the blacking of issue footwear was forbidden.[3]

## Officers

With service dress (i.e. breeches) officers wore high black riding-type boots, which were privately purchased and thus not of standard pattern. Some had plain tops, others had various kinds of straps and buckles around the top to prevent the boot slipping down the calf; boots were either stiff or soft.* Like everything else during the war, boots became increasingly scarce, so that regulations governing the wearing of boots were generally relaxed. In August 1943 Waffen-SS officers were ordered to wear long trousers and ankle boots at all occasions attended by other ranks. With undress uniform (i.e. long trousers) officers wore either black or lacquered leather lace-up or elastic sided ankle boots or shoes.[4] In action and as war progressed, issue marching footwear was increasingly worn with long field-grey trousers by company and field officers.

## Spurs

Officers wore various types of spurs with different orders of dress. With service dress, officers with the rank of SS-Hauptsturmführer and above wore rust-proof, nickel plated spurs with straps and buckles, with either a straight or slightly curved neck and either a sharp or dumb (non-spiked) rowel.[5] With undress uniform they could wear special screw spurs with straight neck and dumb rowel or plain (hunting) neck. For dancing there were special screw dancing spurs (Tanzsporen).[6]

* Although the high black boot (contemptuously misnamed 'jackboot' by the enemies of Germany) became one of the hated symbols of Nazi militarism, there is a touch of irony in the suspicion that the Germans would themselves have held the boot in disrepute after the war on the grounds that its stiff shaft caused varicose veins!

Top: Standard marching boot (Knobelbecher or 'dice shaker') with high shaft.
Bottom: Standard lace-up ankle boot which gradually replaced the costly 'dice shaker'.

35

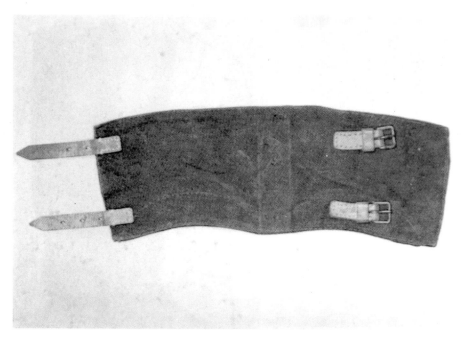

Canvas and leather gaiter for wear with the ankle boot.

It was obvious that many SS officers clanked around in spurs and leather posterior reinforcement to their breeches with no aspirations in horsemanship; nevertheless, throughout its short history there were many SS orders concerning the wearing of spurs. Finally, in June 1943, Himmler issued the following order:

**217. The wearing of spurs.** [7]

The Reichsführer has ordered:

That in the whole SS — Allgemeine, Waffen, and Polizei — only members of mounted or horse drawn units may wear spurs if they are authorised to do so in the relevant regulations.

All other members of the SS and police, officers, N.C.O.s and men of the Allgemeine-SS, Waffen-SS, Order and Security Police may only wear spurs when going to ride, while riding, and on returning from riding.

SS-FHA/Ia

In addition to spurs, there was an adjustable black leather strap (Marschriemen) that fitted under the instep, and around the ankle; it prevented movement of the foot inside the boot when marching.

**Gamaschen**

Gaiters

When leather became scarce in November 1939 the marching boot had to be replaced for economic reasons. In July 1942 a standard lace-up ankle boot was issued in place of the marching boot, to be worn with canvas gaiters in winter and puttees in summer. The gaiters, made of field-grey or olive green canvas with either black or brown leather fittings and binding, were almost identical to those issued to the British army. The gaiter was not a popular innovation and was given a number of disparaging names, such as 'dog blanket' and 'retreat gaiters'; with utmost cunning the German soldier tried to retain his marching boots for as long as possible.

In summer 1943 there was a correspondence between Himmler's adjutant and the head of Department B, SS-Brigaf. Lörner concerning Styrian gaiters (Steirische Übergamaschen). Himmler had approved of them, and wanted them tested in the field by SS-Gebirgs-Division Nord. It is not clear from the correspondence if they were for the exclusive use of mountain troops, or the whole SS, nor is there any description or illustration of the gaiters in question, but it is thought that they are the ones illustrated on p. 51, which appear in many Waffen-SS photographs.

**Abschlussbänder**

Puttees

German puttees were made of an elasticated cloth and were 73 cm long and 8 cm wide with a 20 x 2½ cm strap and patent buckle.

### Wearing of gaiters and puttees

Gaiters were worn over the top of the ankle or ski boot and bottom of the trousers and fastened by two leather straps and metal buckles on the outside so that the straps faced the rear. The correct method of folding the trouser leg was to grasp the back and fold it to the front on the inside. This was to prevent the insides of the trouser legs rubbing together and wearing out.

A popular habit was the rolling of socks outside the trouser leg and over the top of the ankle or ski boot, but this was finally forbidden in August 1944. [8]

### Notes:

1. V.Bl.d.W.-SS., Nr.13, 15 November 1940, Ziff. 335.
2. Ibid. Nr.13, 1 July 1942, Ziff.220.
3. Ibid. Nr.10, 15 May 1944, Ziff.233.
4. SS-Preisliste. Gültig ab 1 November 1940, p. 41 with illustrations.
5. Ibid.
6. Ibid.
7. V.Bl.d.W.-SS., Nr.12, 15 June 1943, Ziff.217.
8. Ibid. Nr.15, 1 August 1944, Ziff.433.

## TARNBEKLEIDUNG

### Camouflage clothing

The design, development, and manufacture of clothing made from a fabric on which a camouflage pattern had been printed was the most original of all SS innovations in the field of uniform and equipment, and was to have an enormous influence on wartime and post-war uniform development. Today most armies in the world wear some form of camouflage clothing.*

Camouflage clothing was tested in the field by SS-Standarte Deutschland in December 1937 and January 1938, and in June 1938, after further investigation by the Reich Patent Office, a patent in respect of each item of clothing was granted to the NSDAP Reichsführer-SS. By 1 November 1938

* Weidinger in his history of the Das Reich division attributes the initiative for the design and development of camouflage clothing and equipment to the commander of the Aufklärungs-Abteilung/SS-VT, SS-Stubaf. Dr.Ing.Brandt. [6] Responsibility for the manufacture of prototypes and initial deliveries rested with Otto Schick, and it was proposed that he and his assistant should be found a post in the inspectorate of the SS-VT. Hausser pointed out that it was unlikely that the army (OKH) would agree, since it was working on standard camouflage clothing for the army and air-force. Hausser thought it would be easier if Schick and his assistant were given an SS post outside the inspectorate. [2]

The first pattern SS camouflage jacket and helmet cover being worn in France, 1940.

SS camouflage smock, 1st pattern.

quantity production of camouflaged groundsheets, steel helmet covers and face masks was already under way.[1]

On 27 January 1939, SS-Brigaf. Hausser reported to the chief of the SS-Hauptamt that despite great difficulties in obtaining sufficient quantities of waterproof cotton duck, and the fact that printing on the material had to be carried out by hand, 8,400 camouflage groundsheets and 6,800 helmet covers had already been supplied to the SS-Verfügungstruppe. It was hoped that the remainder would be supplied by April 1939. Hausser added that he thought it advisable to issue 20 camouflage jackets per company for assault troop training. The face masks he found unusable.[2]

Camouflage clothing was used sparingly during the Polish campaign, and, probably due to Hausser's suggestion, was only issued to assault troops, but this new SS innovation did not go unnoticed by the army. Apparently Generalmajor Werner Kempf, in a report to the Oberkommando des Heeres, praised the camouflage groundsheets and helmet covers used by SS-Standarte Deutschland while under his command. At the request of the OKH the SS agreed to send a sample of the groundsheet and helmet cover to OKH Section In.6, at the Bendlerstrasse, Berlin.[3] The army, however, did not introduce camouflage clothing until 1942/3, and the only other branch of the armed forces to make extensive use of SS camouflage clothing was the air-force General Göring Regiment (later, Hermann Göring Division).

By June 1940 the tedium of hand printing had been superseded by the roller printing press, and the following quantities of camouflage jackets had been delivered:

| | |
|---|---|
| SS-Verfügungs-Division | 10,900 |
| Leibstandarte SS Adolf Hitler | 3,000 |
| SS-Totenkopf-Division | 9,000 |
| SS-Polizei-Division | 9,500 |

By September delivery of a further 30,000 jackets was anticipated, but this would use up the peacetime stock of material. The required quantity of camouflage jackets had been determined by the fact that only field units (divisions) were to be equipped with them, but it was then ordered that the SS Death's Head regiments were also to receive them. It was hoped, however, that 75% of the Death's Head regiments' requirements could be supplied from the 30,000 jackets delivered by September 1940.

The big problem, even at this early date, was raw material supply. Apparently the SS war requirement for waterproof cotton duck had been fixed by the OKH at 42,300 metres per month, but this was only sufficient for 8,500 groundsheets, 6,000 camouflage jackets, and 14,000 steel helmet covers. If groundsheets were not included, then 18,300 sets of jackets and helmet covers could be produced. Pohl hoped to overcome this deficit by getting a larger allocation out of the raw material office at the OKH, and he was confident that if he had sufficient material, any quantity of camouflage items could be manufactured because printing and make-up presented no problems. [4] The original helmet cover, jacket, and face mask were followed, in June 1942, by a camouflage peaked field cap, and in January 1943 by a camouflage combination for armoured vehicle crews. On 9 January Pohl reported that it was now no longer possible to use the high quality cotton duck for camouflage uniforms, and in future the Waffen-SS would have to make do with drill material, which had no waterproofing qualities. As it happened, even drill material was in short supply, and although sufficient for the manufacture of camouflage jackets for the combat strength of existing divisions, no raw materials of any kind would be available for other kinds of camouflage clothing. [5] In fact the jacket was also manufactured from drill material from 1944 until the end of the war.

**Camouflage patterns (see rear end paper)**
As already described, the camouflage pattern was first hand printed, then roller printed in average four colours. The design varied considerably and the general tendency during the war was for an increasingly spotted design in lighter shades. Earlier camouflage uniforms tended to be much darker than later ones.

Most camouflage garments made from waterproof linen duck were printed on both sides, and the articles made from this material were reversible, which was not the case with uniforms made from drill material. On one side the design was predominantly green for wear during the season of maximum foliation, whilst on the reverse it was in various shades of brown for use in autumn, winter, and early spring. There was no significant reason for the difference between one camouflage pattern and another. To suggest, as do some post-war publications, that certain units had special designs, or that special patterns were designed to blend with specific regions in which operations were to take place — or as two British writers suggested in a recent publication on Waffen-SS uniform, that 'there was a special "brick" pattern for wear in predominantly built-up areas' — attributes almost superhuman organisational ability to the supply services of the Waffen-SS.

**Jacket**
The jacket was a smock-like, reversible, pullover garment. It had no collar, and was gathered at the neck, wrists, and waist with elastic. The first pattern had no pockets, but two vertical openings in front, above the waist, which gave the wearer access to his field blouse, which was worn underneath. Wartime modifications to the smock were to sew loops in threes to the front

SS N.C.O. wearing a steel helmet with camouflage cover.

Group of Waffen-SS officers conferring in the field; they wear first pattern camouflage helment covers and smocks. At right, note the applied two-bar sleeve rank badge, denoting a company officer.

A Waffen-SS grenadier wearing the herringbone twill camouflage drill uniform: Hungary, August 1944. (Bundesarchiv).

of the shoulder and upper outside sleeve, and replace the vertical openings with two side pockets with buttoned flaps, below the waist. Some photographs taken towards the end of the war show what appears to be a smock with a collar, but this was in fact the collar of the camouflage field blouse worn underneath the smock during the summer.

The jacket was worn in many different ways. Some personnel tucked the cuffs and skirt of the jacket inside the elastic at the wrist and waist, but in cold weather it was often worn on top of the greatcoat. The jacket appears to have been the only camouflage uniform which seems never to have been worn with insignia. An example in the Imperial War Museum, London, is made of camouflage drill material and modified by a zip fastener fitted in front and the cuffs removed just below the elastic. It ceased to be manufactured in January 1944 with the introduction of the camouflage drill blouse.

### Steel helmet cover

The reversible steel helmet cover in camouflage material for wear on the 1935 model steel helmet began to be introduced in 1939.[2] It was attached to the helmet by three rust-proof, spring-loaded, double-sided metal clips. Helmet covers made from 1942 onwards often had loops sewn onto the front, top, and back of the cover, to hold foliage. The cover was sometimes worn on its own as an improvised camouflage head-dress.

### Face mask

The face mask was one of the original items of camouflage equipment which had undergone trials before the war and was pronounced useless by Hausser in 1939.[2] Since quantities had already been manufactured it was decided to issue them in April 1942.

### 134. New introduction of the camouflaged face mask.[6]

In order to complete the camouflage of men, and in addition to the existing camouflage clothing (jacket and helmet cover) a camouflage face mask will be introduced.

Delivery to the divisions and brigades, etc. of the Waffen-SS will follow. Indents from these units for up to 30% of the fighting strength, for the time being, must be sent to the SS-Wirtschafts-Verwaltungs-Hauptamt, Berlin-Lichterfelde-West, Unter den Eichen 129.

For training purposes each company of Ersatz units will be entitled to two face masks.                                                   SS-FHA/Amt IV

The face mask was basically a series of strings which were fitted to an elasticated strap. At the bottom the strings were woven together, so that they formed a curtain which hung in front of the face. The mask was usually worn on the steel helmet, and when not in use was either thrown back over the helmet or hung round the neck.

The camouflage face-mask.

Top : First pattern camouflage field cap.
Bottom : Camouflage field cap with regulation insignia.

'Panzer-Meyer' as SS-Standartenführer and commander of the 12.SS-Pz. – Div. Hitlerjugend, wearing a field cap and blouse made from Italian camouflage material.

## Field cap

In June 1942, a camouflaged field cap was introduced.[7]

**170. Introduction of a camouflaged field cap for troops.**

The Reichsführer-SS has ordered the introduction of a camouflaged field cap for field units. The cap is to be worn without insignia.

Delivery can begin at the end of May.                    Kdo.d.W.-SS/Ia

The cap was made of waterproof duck, and could be worn with either the autumn or summer pattern on the outside, although the sweat band of the cap was sewn on the autumn side.

**432. Camouflaged field cap.**[8]

By order of the Reichsführer-SS, the field cap will in future be worn with insignia. Existing caps without insignia must be worn out.

SS-FHA/Ia/IV

This necessitated the manufacture of special insignia which were woven in brown artificial silk thread for the autumn, and bright green thread for the summer pattern. The background of the insignia remained black. There were other items of clothing and equipment made from camouflage materials, but these will be dealt with under their respective sections as follows:

| | |
|---|---|
| Groundsheet, | Equipment |
| Combination for tank crews, | Tank uniform |
| Drill uniform, | Drill uniform |
| Drill uniform for tank crews, | Tank uniform |
| Winter uniform, | Winter uniform |
| Parachute smock. | Parachute uniform |

## Non-regulation camouflage uniforms

There are a few recorded instances of Waffen-SS troops wearing camouflage uniforms, other than the standard Waffen-SS pattern. In June 1944 Himmler visited SS-Freiwilligen-Division Galizien in training at Heidelager. Photographs of this visit show Ukrainian volunteers wearing army camouflage smocks and SS camouflage helmet covers.[9] In 1944 large quantities of camouflage uniforms in German cut, but manufactured from Italian camouflage material, appeared in Normandy. There were also isolated cases of Waffen-SS personnel wearing United States camouflage suits in Normandy.

## Notes:

1. J. G. Otto Schick an den Reichsführer-SS.Betr.: Abschluss der Arbeiten für die Tarnausrüstung., München, den 1 November 1938.
2. Der Inspekteur der SS-VT., SS-Brigaf. Hausser an den Chef des SS-Hauptamtes, Inspektion der SS-VT.Betr.: Tarnausrüstung zu

Members of the SS-Heimwehr Danzig wearing the natural coloured herringbone twill drill uniform. Note also the special SS pattern webbing straps supporting, August 1939.

Der Reichsführer-SS, Persönlicher Stab Tgb.Nr.AR/1938/1 Wa./Lü vom 13.12.38. Berlin, den 27 January 1939.

3. Der Chef des Beschaffungsamtes-SS, SS-Oberf. Gärtner an SS-Staf. Diesterweg, Hauptabteilung IX/2, Berlin, den 8 November 1939.
4. SS-Gruf. Pohl, Chef des V.u.W.-Hauptamtes an den Reichsführer. Betr.: Tarniacken, Tarnschirme und Trippelwagen., Berlin, den (?) June 1939.
5. SS-Ogruf.u.Gen.d.W.-SS Oswald Pohl an den Reichsführer-SS Betr.: Bericht über die Rohstofflage auf dem Spinnstoff-und Ledergebiet., Berlin, den 9 January 1943.
6. V.Bl.d.W.-SS., Nr.8, 15 April 1942, Ziff.134.
7. Ibid., Nr.11, 1 June 1942, Ziff.170.
8. Ibid., Nr.23, 1 December 1942, Ziff.432.
9. Die Woche., Nr.23, 7 June 1944, p. 5.

The rush green drill uniform being worn by Bosnian volunteers in the Waffen-SS, January 1944.

## ARBEITSANZUG/DRILLICH
(Working and drill uniform)

At the outbreak of war the armed SS had two basic patterns of drill uniform. The first was the SS-Verfügungstruppe one consisting of a field blouse and long trousers, identical in cut to the field-grey SS field blouse and trousers, but made of a cement coloured herring-bone twill (Drillichstoff). The field blouse was fitted with detachable buttons, shoulder strap loops, and was worn with shoulder straps, national emblem, and collar patches. After the beginning of the war, this blouse was often worn during the summer as a summer uniform.

With the very rapid expansion of the Waffen-SS in 1939–40 it was necessary to issue large quantities of unbleached natural coloured linen herring-bone twill, as used in the German army. The jacket had five detachable buttons in front and two flapless side patch pockets. No insignia was intended to be worn on this jacket. The trousers were the same as their cloth counterpart. During the war the unbleached drill uniform was considered totally impractical because of its colour, and it was either dyed rush green or replaced by one made of rush green linen herring-bone twill. This wartime working uniform included either the Waffen-SS pattern Schiffchen or the standard field cap made of the same material. They differed from cloth models insofar as neither cap had a separate flap which could be lowered. The standard field cap was identical to the one made of camouflage material.

Wartime experience and the need to standardise Waffen-SS uniform brought about the introduction of a combined summer field service and working uniform.

### 99. Camouflaged drill uniform.[1]

To utilise front-line experience, a camouflaged drill uniform consisting of –

Drill blouse . . . Article No. B/40

Drill trousers . . . Article No. B/171

is introduced as a camouflage and working uniform.

On those drill blouses in the same cut as the cloth field blouse, the rank badges for items of clothing without shoulder straps (according to V.Bl.d.W.-SS., Nr.4, 15 February 1943, Ziff.63.) are to be worn 0,5 cm under the national emblem.

Collar patches are not to be worn.

Existing types of drill uniform as well as the camouflage jacket are to be discontinued. Existing stocks may be used up.

SS-FHA/Ia

This uniform was made of unbleached twill on which the camouflage pattern had been printed on one side only, and was therefore not reversible. Insignia, other than the national emblem and special rank badges, were not intended to be worn on the blouse, but there were instances of shoulder straps and other insignia appearing.

    1.  V.Bl.d.W.-SS., Nr.5, 1 March 1944, Ziff.99.

## SS-SPORTBEKLEIDUNG

SS Sports clothes
Sports clothes were purchased from the RZM before the war, but soon after the outbreak of war stocks were reserved for officers and units of the Waffen-SS, who held stocks of sports clothing which was issued as and when required and returned after use. Those members of the Waffen-SS who had been issued with sports clothing before the war continued to use it. In 1941, Waffen-SS troops in Greece used sports clothing as tropical dress, instead of their field-grey field uniform.

SS sports clothing consisted of the following items:[1]

    Shorts, satin, black
    Vest, with SS badge, white
    Training jacket, with SS badge, black
    Training trousers, black
    SS badge for Fencing jacket
    Sports shoes, natural colour, leather

The same items are listed in the March 1941 SS price list, but the training jacket and trousers are described as blue.[2] Sports shoes were included as part of the wartime issue schedule in September 1940.[3]

**Notes:**

    1.  SS-Preisliste, April 1939, p. 3.
    2.  Ibid., p. 3.
    3.  V.Bl.d.W.-SS., Nr.8, 5 September 1940, Ziff.45.

## VARIATIONS ON THE STANDARD FIELD SERVICE UNIFORM

### 1.  Cavalry or horse drawn units.

In addition to long trousers, mounted personnel were issued with a pair of field-grey cloth breeches with seat and inside leg reinforced with grey leather. In place of drill trousers, they received drill breeches. In October 1943[1] standard riding breeches in both cloth and twill were introduced, which had a built-in cloth belt, side and hip pockets with buttons and a fob pocket with flap, and four belt loops at the waist. Instead of marching boots, mounted personnel received a pair of riding boots complete with spurs. Later in the

The 1944 camouflage drill and summer field service uniform.

SS cavalrymen in Russia 1942. It was common practice to tuck the cuffs and skirt of the camouflage smock under the elastic at the wrist and waist.

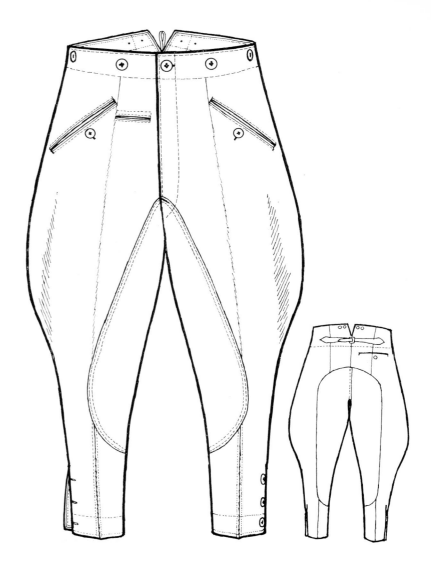

Breeches for mounted personnel.

war mounted personnel made increasing use of ankle boots with puttees or gaiters for training on foot.

## 2. Artillery and Flak (excl. Panzerjäger (anti-tank) and Sturmgeschütz (self-propelled gun) personnel).

Artillery men wore standard field-grey uniform of the Waffen-SS, or with variations for mounted personnel, if they were serving in horse drawn units. During the course of the war various kinds of overalls were worn in action and on maintenance work. In September 1942 anti-aircraft gun crews were issued with black overalls.[2]

### 308. Protective clothing for anti-aircraft gun crews.

For anti-aircraft gun crews serving with field units a two-piece overall consisting of —

Protective jacket, black, drill
(Manufacturer's code B/307)
Protective trousers, black, drill
(Manufacturer's code B/308)
is to be introduced.
Field unit requirements must be forwarded via clothing channels.

Kdo.d.W.-SS/Ia

## 3. Engineers

Engineers also wore standard field-grey uniform (Black special clothing if crews of armoured vehicles in Panzer-Pioniere units), but because of their specialised tasks they wore many kinds of protective clothing and equipment, such as rubber waders for bridge building and life jackets for crossing rivers; these articles were neither clothing or personal equipment but technical apparatus issued for the task in hand.

## 4. Mountain units

Before the war great importance was attached to the training of SS personnel in mountainous regions and winter sports, for which purpose the following black, (for Allgemeine-SS) and earth-grey (for SS-Verfügungstruppe) ski clothing had been introduced in 1938:[3]

    Ski cap, gabardine, black or earth-grey
    Ski blouse, gabardine, black or earth-grey
    Ski trousers, gabardine, black or earth grey
    Puttees

Before the war ski clothing was issued to personnel only for the duration of training, then returned to stores, but in 1940 Waffen-SS units serving in Norway were already being issued with suitable clothing and equipment for wear in mountainous regions.

The black overall for crews of anti-aircraft guns, Russia winter 1942-3.

**Bekleidung und Ausrüstung der Einheiten im Gebirgsdienst.**
Clothing and equipment of units in mountain service

**418. Clothing and equipment of units in mountain service.** [4]

1. Following the order of the SS-Führungshauptamt — IVa/14a/10.40 — of 23 October 1940, units of the Waffen-SS stationed in Norway and issued with mountain equipment, are to receive the following new items:

(a) **Clothing**
1. Mountain blouse, grey
2. Mountain cap, grey
3. Mountain cap cover
4. Wind cheater
5. Mountain trousers, grey
6. Snow smock
7. Pullover for mountain troops
8. Mittens (to go over gloves)
9. Mountain boots
10. Wrist warmers
11. Winter undervest
12. Winter underpants
13. Woollen scarf

(b) **Equipment**
14. Rucksack with carrying straps
15. Water-bottle, large capacity

2. For units in mountain service* the following alterations are to be made to the order of the Hauptamt für Haushalt und Bauten, Amt KJ I/3 M 204/3 of 11 November 1939, and the following obligatory clothing and equipment is laid down:

| | Article | Quantity |
|---|---|---|
| 5. | Mountain trousers, grey | 1 |
| 1. | Mountain blouse, grey | 1 |
| 16. | Cloth trousers, long, grey | 1 |
| 17. | Greatcoat, grey | 1 |
| 2. | Mountain cap, grey | 1 |
| 3. | Mountain cap cover | 1 |
| 18. | Field cap | 1 |

*During the first disastrous Russian winter (1941–2) all available mountain troop winter clothing was issued to field units, this applied particularly to the snow smock.

| | | |
|---|---|---|
| 19. | Drill blouse | 1 |
| 20. | Drill trousers | 1 |
| 9. | Mountain boots | 1 |
| 21. | Ankle boots, lace-up | 1 |
| 4. | Wind cheater | 1 |
| 6. | Snow smock 10% of strength | |
| 22. | Undershirt | 2 |
| | or | |
| 23. | Brown shirt, trikot | 3 |
| 24. | Collar liner | 2 |
| | or | |
| 25. | Black tie | 2 |
| 26. | Underpants | 2 |
| 12. | Winter underpants | 2 (W) |
| 7. | Pullover for mountain troops | 1 (W) |
| 13. | Woollen scarf | 1 (W) |
| 27. | Socks, thick (Überstrümpfe), pr. | 1 (W) |
| 28. | Knitted head defender | 1 (W) |
| 8. | Mittens (to go over gloves) | 1 (W) |
| 29. | Gloves, wool | 1 (W) |
| 30. | Socks, prs. | 3 |
| 31. | Body belt (every third man) | 1 |
| 32. | Braces | 1 |
| 33. | Handkerchiefs | 3 |
| 10. | Wrist warmers, pr. | 1 |

**Equipment**

| | | |
|---|---|---|
| 14. | Rucksack with carrying straps | 1 |
| 34. | Greatcoat straps | 3 |
| 35. | Groundsheet and accessories consisting of: | 1 |
| | 1 groundsheet | |
| | 1 line | |
| | 1 peg | |
| | 2 poles | |
| 36. | Steel helmet, complete | |
| 37. | Clothing bag | 1 |
| 38. | Waist belt | 1 |
| 39. | Waist belt buckle | 1 |
| 40. | Bayonet frog | 1 |
| 41. | Ammunition pouches | 2 |

| Article | Quantity |
|---|---|
| 42. Bread bag | 1 |
| 43. Bread bag strap | 1 |
| 44. Mess-tin | 1 |
| 45. Eating implements | 1 |
| 46. Identity disc with cord | 1 |
| 47. Dust- and sun-glasses | 1 |
| 48. Towel | 1 |
| 49. Carrying straps for blouse | 2 |
| 50. Steel side hooks | 4 |
| 51. Sewing bag | 1 |
| 52. Cleaning brushes, set | 1 |
| (W) = Issued only in winter | |

It is not intended here to describe the exact function and manufacture of every article listed above, since this would require a manual on mountaineering, so it is only possible to describe those items of clothing which differed considerably from standard pattern. Equipment will be covered in the section dealing with that subject.

2. In the above listing, the mountain cap is included in addition to the field cap (Schiffchen), because at the time it was still classified as an item of special clothing for wear when mountaineering. It had not yet become a distinctive head-dress. Being an issue item it was identical for all ranks, although officers could buy extra caps of superior quality, often with aluminium piping around the crown *and* on the front of the flap. The field cap was worn in barracks and on field training when the steel helmet was not specified. In March 1941 the mountain cap was officially recognised as a distinctive head-dress. [5]

## 306. SS Mountain cap.

The Reichsführer-SS has authorised all members of
SS-Gebirgs-Division Nord and SS-Freiwilligen-Division Prinz Eugen
to wear the mountain cap.

The Reichsführer-SS has forbidden all officers, N.C.O.s and men in other units from wearing the mountain cap.

Kdo.d.W.-SS/Ia

Mountain troop officers in typical service dress 1943. Three of the officers wear ski trousers, while the one in the middle wears plus fours and knitted woollen socks. It is interesting to note that all four ski caps bear different insignia; L-R woven national emblem and death's head in front and SS edelweiss on the left; metal death's head in front and metal army edelweiss on left; metal death's head in front, woven death's head in front and national emblem on the left.

SS mountain troops with heavily loaded rucksacks and the special large capacity water bottle.

But in September 1943 it was decided to introduce a standard field cap for the whole Waffen-SS, to be modelled on the mountain cap, and it was therefore necessary to preserve the special identity of Waffen-SS mountain troops by the introduction, in October 1943, of the cloth edelweiss for wear on the left side of the standard field cap and mountain cap. (For details of the insignia and method of wearing see Vol. 7 of the present series.)

3.   In winter a white knitted woollen cover was worn over the mountain cap, and in the forests of Lappland the steel helmet cover was worn either on top of the mountain cap or on its own as camouflage head-dress, and this practice may well have been responsible for the introduction of a camouflaged field cap later in the war. [6]

4.   The army pattern wind cheater is included in the above listing, although photographs of it being worn by Waffen-SS personnel have not so far come to light. This double-breasted, 10-button, olive green calico jacket, had two slanting pockets with buttoned flaps above the waist, and two patch side pockets with centre pleats and buttoned flaps. It had a half belt at the back with two buttons, and the cuffs could be fastened tightly around the wrist by means of a tab and button. All buttons, except those for the shoulder straps, which were in metal, were either horn or plastic. Only insignia normally worn on this garment were the shoulder straps.

5.   Field-grey mountain trousers were cut wider in the leg than standard long trousers, and were reinforced in the seat. The trouser legs were fastened at the ankle by draw-strings and held inside the mountain boot by foot straps. In 1943 mountain trousers were gradually replaced by the new Keilhose. [7] Popular with mountaineers were the non-regulation climbing trousers or knickerbockers, which were buckled just under the knee and worn with long woollen socks.

6.   The snow smock or shirt was a loose fitting single-breasted undyed cotton smock, designed to be worn over the normal uniform and equipment as camouflage in snowy terrain. It was fitted with a hood and collar, and had two vertical slits above the waist to enable the wearer to reach his blouse pockets or ammunition pouches. Buttons were standard metal pattern with matt-white finish.

8.   Canvas mittens with leather palms and wrist straps were used in conjunction with woollen gloves to improve insulation and keep the gloves dry.

9.   Boots had a specially designed lace-up ankle and thick studded soles for climbing and skiing. Many officers and mountaineers wore their own

privately purchased mountain footwear, which did not conform to any standard pattern. Mountaineers also wore special rock climbing canvas ankle boots with rope or felt soles.

10. Wrist warmers were made of field-grey, bottle green or grey knitted wool, and were 10 cm long and open at both ends. They were designed to seal off the sleeve at the wrist to exclude draughts and protect the wrist where the sleeve and glove joined.

49. On the outside of the field blouse at waist level, four sets of three (later two) holes can be seen in front and at the back. These were designed to take a metal hook of special design, which on the inside was attached to a fabric strap which formed part of the blouse lining. The strap was designed to take a hook, and distribute the fully loaded weight of the waist belt throughout the shoulders of the field blouse.

50. Mountain troops were often called upon to carry considerable weights and it was found necessary to reinforce these fabric straps by two 94 cm long webbing ones (Tragegurte). The metal hooks were attached to the ends of the straps, which were then worn over the shoulder inside the blouse. By supporting the hooks the straps transferred the burden to the wearer's shoulders and thus relieved the strain on the blouse.

The following items are known to have been issued, subsequent to these lists. At the end of 1942 a new anorak and overalls began to replace the wind cheater in the army, and was soon issued to Waffen-SS personnel. The anorak and overalls were made of a special reversible rayon, white on one side and tan or rush green on the other, which had excellent waterproofing qualities when wet and good insulation when dry.

Initially neither puttees nor gaiters appear to have been worn by Waffen-SS mountain troops, and the trousers were held inside the mountain boot by a footstrap. Eventually short, elasticated army-style puttees (Wickelgamaschen) were issued (measuring 73 x 8 cm, with a $20\frac{1}{2}$ x $2\frac{1}{2}$ cm strap) which secured trousers and top of the boot and gave added ankle support. Meanwhile the Waffen-SS was developing its own type of gaiters based on the old Austrian army 'Styrian' pattern. In June 1943 Himmler requested that ten pairs of four different patterns be sent to SS-Gebirgs-Division Nord for field evaluation.[8] The gaiters, made from various types and colours of canvas, covered the top of the boot and laced on the outside. Straps and binding were made of webbing. A combined webbing and metal footstrap, is one feature which suggests that these gaiters were primarily designed for use by mountain troops, since a webbing or leather strap would have been severed by the metal studs and nails affixed to the soles of mountain boots.

Top: Standard issue mountain boot.
Bottom: Mountain boot with 'Styrian gaiter'.

51

A Bosnian Moslem being issued with brand-new mountain troop clothing, 1942.

**Notes:**
1. V.Bl.d.W.-SS, Nr.19, 1 October 1943, Ziff.357.
2. Ibid. Nr.17, 1 September 1942, Ziff.308.
3. SS-Preisliste., Nr.3, 1 January 1938.
4. V.Bl.d.W.-SS., Nr.14, 1 December 1940, Ziff.418.
5. Ibid. Nr.17, 1 September 1942, Ziff. 306.
6. Kampf unter dem Nordlicht. Illustration between pp. 176 and 177.
7. V.Bl.d.W.-SS., Nr.19, 1 October 1943, Ziff.357.
8. Der Chef des Amtes B II, SS-Wirtschafts und Verwaltungshauptamt SS-Brigaf.Lörner an SS-Ostubaf.Dr.Brandt (Pers.Stab. RF-SS)., Berlin, 28 June 1943.

## 5. Training and replacement units.

Before the war it was normal practice to issue a new recruit with one complete field service uniform for wear during basic training, on completion of which he was issued with a second set. The first, now somewhat worn and often stripped of insignia was relegated for wear in barracks, while the new uniform was reserved for wear on exercises and manoeuvres outside barracks.

Even before the war and the rapid expansion of the Waffen-SS, the first everyday uniform, or part of it, consisted of odd items of the old earth-grey service uniform, until finally withdrawn in March 1941.[1] Already by 1939 training and replacement units were being issued with the most unusual selection of uniforms for their basic training. Members of the SS-Totenkopf-Ergänzungssturmbann III in Breslau, for example, were wearing First World War tunics of the Leib-Kürassier-Regt. Nr.1, with black collar and white litzen, for stable duty and training, without SS insignia. During the Polish campaign they were referred to by the German army as the 'strange guards'.[2] By 1940 most training and replacement personnel were being issued with two field-grey field uniforms and a set of drill. As raw materials became scarce and stocks depleted, Ersatz units were the first to suffer; in 1941 they were no longer issued with marching boots but two pairs of ankle boots.[3] By the end of the war the Waffen-SS was not even able to issue the two basic sets of field and one set of drill uniform, and were forced to requisition stocks of miscellaneous uniforms, or manufacture new sets out of whatever materials were available. In 1944–5 members of the Feldersatz battalions of the Totenkopf and Wiking divisions in Schröttersburg (Weichsel) were wearing field blouses made out of two different kinds and colours of material. The breast and back portions (above the waist) were made of dark drill material, while the lower part of the front and back portions (below the waist), collar and sleeves, were made of the normal field-grey material. The greatcoats were earth-brown.[4] Many a young SS recruit, attracted by the glamour and appeal of the SS uniform, must have suffered severe disillusionment as he stared at the motley collection of 'hand-me-downs' with which he was issued on reporting for service.

## Notes:

1. V.Bl.d.W.-SS. Nr.4, 1 March 1941, Ziff. 121.
2. Der Freiwillige. Nr.1, January 1970, pp. 16-17.
3. V.Bl.d.W.-SS., Nr.20, 1 November 1941, Ziff.428.
4. Feldgrau., Nr.1, January 1956, p. 19.

## BEKLEIDUNG DER PANZEREINHEITEN
Clothing of armoured units

The German definition of the term armoured troops for the purpose of issuing the special tank black uniform, was the crew and exchange crew of tanks, armoured cars, and radio vehicles with enclosed superstructures. All other personnel in armoured units wore the standard field-grey uniform. Towards the end of the war there was a tendency to issue the special black uniform to all personnel in an armoured unit.

The special black uniform was first introduced in 1938 for wear when on duty with an armoured vehicle, since dirt and grease marks would not show up. With other orders of dress the standard field-grey uniform was normally worn. Later in the war the black uniform was proudly worn at every opportunity, even when walking-out on Reich territory. In fact this was due to field-grey uniforms being no longer issued in addition to the black. At first the special black SS uniform was manufactured by the SS Clothing Works and differed slightly from its army counterpart, but once again rapid expansion necessitated the issue of army uniform. In complete contrast to the situation which came about with the field-grey SS field uniform, the SS managed to maintain the supplies of its own special black uniform, and it is therefore rare to see the army pattern being worn after 1942. As in the army, there was no special black greatcoat to go with this uniform, and standard field-grey was issued.

## Schutzmütze/Baskenmütze
Crash helmet

This special head-dress was designed to act both as a protective head-dress and a smart item of military uniform. It consisted of a round black cloth headpiece,* padded with rubber and lined with American cloth, with four rubber ventilation holes. Over the headpiece fitted a large black felt beret.

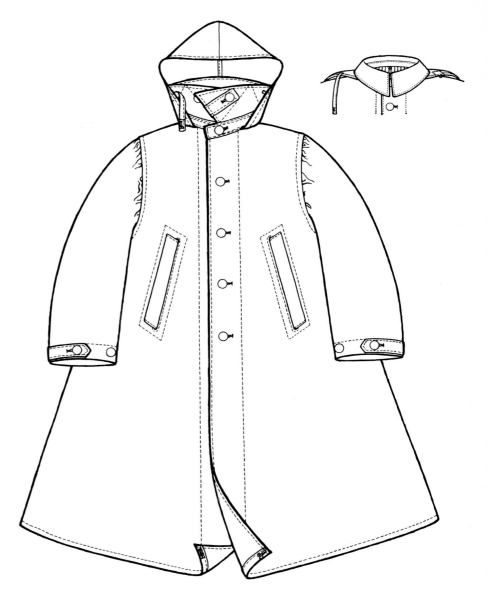

Snow smock with detail of collar.

Armoured car crews from the SS Reconnaissance Battalion in the SS version of the special black clothing, France 1940

On the front of the beret were worn special versions of the national emblem and death's head, both of which were machine-embroidered in silver grey silk thread on a black ground. This issue item of head-dress was identical for all ranks. However, the beret was withdrawn after proving impractical during combat experience; in its place, either the Schiffchen, standard field cap in black cloth (see section on head-dress), or the steel helmet were worn.

## Feldjacke
### Field jacket

This was a short double-breasted black jacket fastened with seven black plastic buttons, with collar worn open or closed with brown shirt (later grey-green) and black tie. It differed from its army counterpart insofar as the front was cut vertically instead of slanting, and had much shorter lapels. Jackets were also privately made from various lightweight or camouflage materials.[1] The collar of the black jacket was sometimes piped in pink for other ranks, and either pink piping or twisted aluminium cord for officers. It has been suggested that pink piping was only worn by members of the SS Pz. Regt.5 (Wiking Div.),[2] but this is not confirmed by photographic evidence.[3] It is more likely that early in the war army field jackets with pink piping were in fact worn by both officers and men without regard to the unit. Aluminium twisted cord on the collar was traditionally worn by SS officers, and appears to have been worn by most on the black field jacket.

Collar patches for other ranks were also piped in pink, but again photographic evidence does not limit it to members of Aufkl.Abt.5, as photographs of it worn by members of the Aufkl.Abt.LSSAH.1 do exist. It is most likely that pink piping was originally intended to identify members of reconnaissance battalions from those in Panzer regiments, but this fine distinction, like many others, became blurred in wartime.

N.C.O.s (with the possible exception of those in Pz.Rgt.LSSAH.1.) did not wear lace on the collar of the black field jacket.

*The base of the Panzer beret had a second lease of life when existing stocks were covered with tan material and, fitted with rabbit fur flaps, issued as winter head-dress.

### Notes:

1. Die Deutsche Wehrmacht 1934 bis 1945. Heft.12 with illustration.
2. The Waffen-SS, its divisional insignia, p. 22.
3. See for example the photo of Max Wünsche as SS-Stubaf., and Chef I./SS.Pz.Rgt.LSSAH.1., in Bender–Taylor Vol. 1, p. 44. This quite clearly shows pink piping.

**Feldhose**
Field trousers
These were similar to the army pattern, having slanting side pockets with flap and button (later two buttons), watch pocket, and buttoned hip pocket. They were baggy and cut like ski trousers, the bottoms fastened around the ankle by draw-strings and footstraps.

**Fussbekleidung**
Footwear
Originally both marching and lace-up ankle boots were issued with the black uniform, but from 1941[1], ankle boots and gaiters only were to be worn, although it appears this order was disregarded and those in possession of marching boots continued to wear them.
In August 1941 the need for a practical working and summer uniform, and the necessity to provide reconnaissance personnel with a less conspicuous uniform when operating on foot brought about the introduction of the reed green drill uniform.

### 355. Protective clothing for personnel in armoured reconnaissance units.[2]

1.  Crews of armoured cars are to be issued with protective clothing in the same cut and make-up as the black field uniform. This protective clothing is to be worn as camouflage over the black uniform, or on its own in summer, and also to protect the black uniform.
    Designation and article number:
    Field jacket, drill, reed green,
        for tanks . . . Article No. 309;
    Field trousers, drill, reed-green,
        for tanks . . . Article No. 310.

2.  The drill uniform for these units is discontinued.

3.  Divisional requirements must be sent to the SS-Verwaltungsamt with the next clothing indent.

                                        V3/431/8.41.

Although the basic cut of the jacket and trousers remained unchanged, there were minor modifications, such as a large patch pocket with flap and button added to the left front of the jacket and left thigh of the trousers. In January 1943, the reed green drill uniform was replaced by a new one-piece reversible camouflage combination. The old reed green drill uniform continued to be worn, and was still in use in Normandy in June 1944.

Machine embroidered badges for the Panzer beret. The national emblem is often mistaken for the sleeve emblem but was of special design.

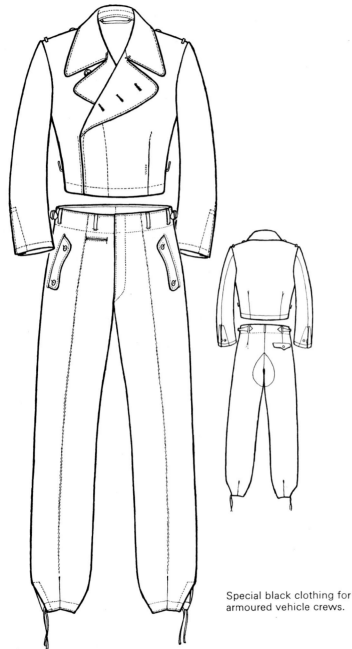

Special black clothing for
armoured vehicle crews.

### 26. Camouflage combination for tank crews. [3]

V.Bl.d.W.-SS., Nr.16, 1 September 1941, Ziff.355

1. The crews and exchange crews of tanks, armoured cars, and radio vehicles with enclosed armoured superstructures are to be issued with a camouflage combination instead of the protective clothing, drill, reed green.
2. Designation and article Number:
   Combination, camouflaged, for tanks . . . Article No. 306.
3. Field unit requirements must be forwarded to the WVHA.

SS-FHA./a/Amt IV.

The combination was made of water repellent cotton duck with autumn and summer shade camouflage patterns. It was usually issued with the national emblem on the left sleeve, shoulder strap loops and detachable metal shoulder strap buttons. Later models had a large patch pocket with flap and button on the front of the left thigh. Nevertheless, the need to provide crews with better winter clothing was anticipated.

### 27. Winter combination for tank crews. [4]

In order to improve the winter clothing of tank crews and exchange crews, a new combination is introduced.

Designation and article number:

Winter combination for tanks . . . Article No. 396.

Field unit requirements must be forwarded to the WVHA.

SS-FHA./Ia/Amt.IV)

The winter combination was basically the same cut as the camouflaged one, but was made of two thicknesses of cloth, white on one side, and field-grey on the other.

Because of the difficulty in getting in and out of a combination, it was never very popular, and so in January 1944, it was decided to re-issue the two-piece drill uniform in camouflage material instead of reed-green. This was also done to coincide with the introduction in the rest of the Waffen-SS of the camouflage working and summer field service uniform. [5]

### Unofficial uniforms

On the whole the clothing of armoured personnel appears to have been fairly standard, but there were two major changes at divisional level, both of which took place in Normandy in 1944. The first was the wearing of various items of camouflage clothing, field caps, jackets, and combinations by members of the Hitlerjugend and its parent Adolf Hitler Division, which were made from Italian camouflage material. [6] The Adolf Hitler Division arrived in

SS-Stubaf. Mühlenkamp (Kdr. SS-Pz. Rgt. 5) after the award of the Knight's Cross, Russia, September 1943. This shows a good cross-section of Panzer troop clothing.

Captured SS men wearing the rush green drill uniform for armoured vehicle crews, Normandy June 1944.

France in December 1943 after helping disarm the Italian armed forces and fighting partisans in northern Italy, and provided a cadre for the formation of the Hitlerjugend Division. Large quantities of Italian motor transport and other materials were used to replace disastrous German shortages.[7] In Italian naval depots large quantities of German leather U-boat clothing (originally supplied by Germany to Italy) were discovered, requisitioned, and issued to German tank crews in Normandy.[8]

**Notes:**
1. V.Bl.d.W.-SS., Nr.13, 1 July 19, Ziff.220.
2. Ibid., Nr.16, 1 September 1941, Ziff.355.
3. Ibid., Nr.2, 15 January 1943, Ziff.26.
4. Ibid.
5. Ibid., Nr.5, 1 March 1944, Ziff. 99.
6. See illustration on p. 42.
7. Die Waffen-SS., pp. 181–3.
8. Verbal conversation with the former divisional Ordnance Officer February 1972.

## FELDGRAUE SONDERBEKLEIDUNG
Field-grey special clothing
The special field-grey clothing was first issued to members of the Sturmgeschütz-Batterie LSSAH in time for the campaign in the Balkans in the summer of 1941, but it was not until August 1942 that it was issued to crews of self-propelled guns (Sturmgeschütze).

### 283. Special clothing for assault gun units.[1]
Assault gun crews will be equipped with the newly introduced special clothing.
Field jacket, field-grey
(Prod. code 311, subject B)
and
Field trousers, field-grey
(Prod. code 314, subject B)
Existing field blouses and trousers will be worn out. In accordance with the published order (V.Bl.d.W.-SS., Nr.16., 1 September 1941, Ziff.348) non-mounted personnel are issued with one pair of ankle boots instead of the marching boots with ordinary uniform.

Kdo.d.W.-SS/Ia

In December 1942 the wearing of the field grey special clothing was also extended to self-propelled anti-tank gun units (Panzerjägereinheiten.(Sfl.).[2] The uniform consisted of a field-grey jacket and long trousers, brown shirt

The camouflage Panzer combination, Russia summer 1943.

'Panzermeyer' wearing the reversible winter combination for tank crews, during the battle of Charkov, February/March 1943.

SS-Panzerschütze during the battle of Normandy wearing the camouflage drill uniform for tank crews.

Black leather U-boat clothing being worn by members of the 2/Pz. Regt. 12 (Hitlerjugend Division) near Rheims, November 1943.

(later field-grey) and black tie. Although not mentioned in the above order a field-grey version of the black beret was also produced,[3] but it was not worn until the introduction in 1943 of a self-propelled rocket launcher with enclosed superstructure (Maultier Sd.Kfz.3). Officers usually wore the issue field uniform with their badges of rank. N.C.O.s (with the exception of those in SS-Sturmgesch.Abt. and SS Pz.Jäg.Abt LSSAH.1.) did not wear lace on the jacket collar.[4] Pink piping was worn on the collar by certain members of Pz.Jäg battalions, and a few officers wore twisted aluminium cord, but recorded cases of these practices are rare.

**Notes:**
1. V.Bl.d.W.-SS., Nr.16, 15 August 1942, Ziff.283.
2. Ibid., Nr.23, 1 December 1942, Ziff.434.
3. There is an example of a field-grey beret with insignia in the collection of David Delich, Kansas City, Ohio, U.S.A.

## FALLSCHIRM-SONDERBEKLEIDUNG
Parachute clothing
Of all the branches of the SS, least is known about the clothing and equipment of SS parachutists. SS troops took part in two well-known airborne operations—the liberation of Mussolini and the attempted capture of Tito in his mountain HQ in Yugoslavia. Despite these events there is little or no reference to the clothing and equipment of the troops who participated in the operations.[1]
It appears that the air-force assumed responsibility not only for their parachute training and transportation by air, but also the equipping of SS parachutists with special air-force clothing and equipment. Normally then SS parachutists wore standard field-grey uniform with the parachutist helmet instead of the standard 1935 model. The best method of ascertaining exactly what they wore is to analyse existing photographs of them.

### Liberation of Mussolini, Gran Sasso, Italy, 12 September 1943.
SS-Sturmbannführer Skorzeny and his small glider-borne SS commando wore German air-force tropical clothing with air-force national emblem on the head-dress, shirt, and field blouse, and Waffen-SS shoulder straps. Skorzeny himself wore a Waffen-SS steel helmet. Leather equipment, such as the sub machine-gun pouches appear to have been the early SS leather pattern. At a rally in the Berlin Sports Palace after the rescue, Otto Skorzeny and members of his commando wore field-grey Waffen-SS service dress.

### Raid on Tito's Headquarters, Drvar, Yugoslavia, 25 May 1944.
On this operation (Rösselsprung) two companies of SS parachutists, from SS-Fallschirmjäger-Bataillon 500, were dropped by parachute and two landed by glider. The parachutists under the command of SS-Hauptsturm-

Three N.C.O.'s from the SS-Pz. Jäg. Abt. 'LSSAH', Spring 1943 in Russia. They are all wearing the special field-grey clothing. Only N.C.O.s in this division were permitted to wear lace on the collar of this jacket. The 'Spiess' in the centre wears an army national emblem and tank troop death's head on his field cap.

61

SS paratroopers during the raid on Tito's HQ, Drvar, Yugolsavia May 1944.

führer Rybka, wore air-force clothing and equipment. It consisted of steel helmet (with or without camouflage net), geometric pattern camouflage smock, complete with air-force national emblem on the right breast,* field-grey trousers with the side opening thigh pockets, canvas gaiters, and ankle boots. SS uniform was represented by the field cap (Schiffchen) with SS insignia and the belt buckle.

Towards the end of the war, SS, like air-force parachutists, were thrown into action as infantry, and continued to wear standard field-grey clothing and the parachutists helmet.

> \*   Recently a batch of brand new (one only worn) parachutists smocks, made of SS camouflage drill material with the SS national emblem on the right breast, turned up in America. According to unconfirmed reports these were found by American troops in the SS Clothing Depot at Dachau in April 1945. They were brought back to America, like so much SS camouflage clothing, because they were thought to be ideal for duck shooting. This is the only recorded instance of the SS national emblem sewn on the right breast, and may have had something to do with the status of SS parachutists under air-force operational command.

## SCHUTZANZUG
Protective clothing
Protective clothing was issued to Waffen-SS personnel, irrespective of their branch of service, to protect their ordinary clothing and person from severe climatic and physical conditions, but which cannot be classified as winter clothing.

## Kradschutzmantel
Motor-cyclist's coat
This was first introduced for army dispatch riders and personnel in units equipped with motor-cycles, and later adopted by the SS, and worn by all branches of the armed forces, Waffen-SS and police until the end of the war. The coat was made of a rubberised fabric, but like the greatcoat, also had at first a dark green cloth collar, but already in 1939 coats with field-grey cloth collars were in use.[1] The coat was double breasted with wide sleeves that

## Notes:
1. In April 1944 it was announced that only those who were physically suitable could wear parachute clothing. This excluded those with large thighs and thick torsos. V.Bl.d.W.-SS., Nr.8, 15 April 1944, Ziff.189.

SS paratroopers smock.

Late version of the air-force parachutist's steel helmet, as issued to SS paratroopers.

Dispatch rider wearing the rubberised motor cyclist's coat, and brown leather gauntlets with seperated thumb and forefinger.

could be fastened tightly around the wrist. The skirt of the coat could be divided and buttoned around the legs. Although originally intended as a motor-cycling coat, it proved popular as a raincoat and often worn as such by Waffen-SS personnel. The rubberised material was not very strong and did not stand up well to the rigours of front-line use, so the following order was issued:

### 216. Motor-cyclist's coat.[1]
The motor-cyclist's coat may only be worn on duty by members of the Waffen-SS, who have been officially issued with it. The motor-cyclist's coat must be worn over the equipment. Only when action is imminent may the belt be worn over the coat.

SS-FHA/Ia

In addition to the coat, overalls were made of the same material, and designed to be worn over both the ordinary trousers and footwear during wet or muddy conditions. Other specialised protective clothing for motor-cyclists were various types of goggles with either normal or smoked anti-glare and sun lenses, and either gauntlets or mittens in canvas or leather. The gauntlets were made of a dark brown leather and had a separate thumb and forefinger, and could be fastened at the wrist with an adjustable strap and press studs.

### Note:
1. V.Bl.d.W.-SS., Nr.3, 1 February 1943, Ziff.216.

### WINTERBEKLEIDUNG
Winter clothing
It is well known that the Germans hoped to defeat Russia before the coming of winter, and therefore made little or no preparations for waging winter warfare. Failure to provide troops with adequate warm clothing resulted in disaster. For the average German winter, a pullover, knitted woollen gloves, greatcoat, and toque were considered sufficient additional clothing for troops able to return and sleep in modern quarters; after the campaigns of 1940, extra winter clothing had to be provided for troops serving in Norway.

### 419. Special clothing for especially cold zones.[1]
1. The following items are introduced as additional winter clothing for especially cold zones:
   Anorak with hood, fur lined.
   Fur waistcoat.
   These articles will only be considered for units quartered in former Polish territory and Norway. The anorak is not suitable for cavalry units, and so is not provided. These units will be issued with sheepskins.

2. The entitlement is:
    Anorak with hood, fur lined for 10% of the fighting strength.
    Fur waistcoat, one per man.
The anorak with hood is to be used for patrols over fairly long distances.
The guard coat, fur, is intended for stationary or walking guard duty
within the area of the barracks.
Allocation will be made on procurement, and according to available
stocks by application to the Verwaltungsamt der Waffen-SS.
Units in Norway will be given priority in supplies.

V/3 431/December 1940

### Pelzweste

Fur waistcoat

This was a short (just below the waist) sleeveless waistcoat designed
for wear under the greatcoat for additional warmth, and was made from
any available types of fur and to no standard pattern.

### Windbluse mit Kapuze, pelz-gefüttert

Fur lined anorak

It is not known whether this was the same as the garment that appeared
during the winter of 1942–3, but it is considered unlikely. So far it has not been
possible to identify this item in photographs.

### Nacktpelz

Sheepskins

The version intended for use by mounted units was a three-quarter length
double-breasted sheepskin coat with lamb's wool collar.

### Wachmantel

Guard coat

This was a traditional garment for sentries on static guard duty in extreme
cold. The coat was made of sheepskin with lamb's wool collar, and was very
long — almost touching the ground. It was usually worn together with straw
over boots.

During the first Russian winter of 1941–2 German troops were forced to
augment their meagre winter clothing with whatever they could lay their
hands on, and improvise as best they could. The items listed above were made
available whenever possible, and often two greatcoats were issued, worn
one on top of the other. But the greatcoat and surcoat were not very practical
for wear in action, and weight alone imposed quite a burden on the wearer.
Stocks of clothing originally intended for mountain troops, such as woollen
scarves, mittens, winter underwear, and most important of all, the snow
smock, were issued to the fighting troops whenever possible. Where shortages

Winter clothing issued to Estonian volunteers near Leningrad, December 1942. The
hooded white cotton smock was primarily for camouflage, and was worn over other
types of warm winter clothing. The boots were made of white canvas with leather
binding and rubber soles.

An unidentified SS officer wearing one of the many different patterns of sheepskin cap and coat which were made for the SS in Poland and Russia.

were still apparent, captured Russian winter clothing, particularly caps, were issued. Sheepskin clothing, the traditional Russian peasant winter clothing, was either requisitioned from or manufactured by the Russians themselves, and either sold or bartered to the Germans.

In Germany a massive collection of winter clothing was instituted, and thousands of ladies' old fur coats, rusty skis, and old toboggans were rushed to the front, often without repair or alteration. Nevertheless, the wretched supply situation at the front was not alleviated until winter had brought much suffering, hardship, and death to many ill-equipped troops.

In April 1942 winter clothing was re-collected for repair and storage until further need.[2] Throughout 1942 the Waffen-SS developed and manufactured its own winter combat clothing independent of the army. It consisted of a fur-lined pullover anorak in a water repellent, cement coloured gabardine, lined with various kinds of black, brown, or white furs, or sheepskin. Overalls were unlined and unquilted, and designed to be worn over ordinary trousers. The bottoms of the trousers finished in a gaiter, which fitted over the top of the boot with laces and footstraps; by this time the lace-up ankle boot was in general use, and the gaiter prevented melted snow from entering the boot. When snow lay on the ground, an undyed cotton overall, consisting of a separate smock with hood and trousers (specially designed to go over anorak and trousers) was issued. The advantage of this arrangement was that the white over garments tended to get very dirty but being separable could be easily cleaned or replaced.

Head-dress consisted of a fur cap, based roughly on the Russian model, with ear flaps. The head piece was usually made of leather, sheepskin, field-grey cloth, or the same material as the anorak. Another pattern utilised existing stocks of Panzer berets by covering the black head piece with cement coloured cloth and fitting rabbit fur to the front and ear flaps. This may have been originally intended for crews of armoured vehicles, as photographs of it being worn are very rare.

### 330. Issue of winter clothing.[3]

From 15 September 1942 all units must be issued with articles of winter clothing:

Woollen gloves
Balaclava helmet
Surcoat
Gauntlets or mittens } For drivers only
Pullover
Over socks

Requirements of these articles are to be forwarded to the competent service offices.

Fur clothing and other special winter clothing* is not issued to Ersatz units. The provision of the field reserve (Feldersatz) with these articles will be undertaken in due course through collecting points, possibly Riga, Stettin, Warschau and Kracau. There will be further instructions. Existing stocks from the fur and textile collections by the German people are to be issued on transfer to the front as additional clothing, and a simultaneous entry to that effect is to be made in the pay book.

The additional issue of a second army blanket or greatcoat is not permissible. Field units will be supplied with winter clothing by a special regulation of the SS-Wirtschafts-Verwaltungshauptamt.

SS-FHA/IV

## Kopfschützer
Balaclava helmet/toque

This was basically an open ended cylinder of knitted wool (measuring 33 x 29 cm) which could be worn in a number of different ways — round the neck like a scarf, on the head like a cap comforter, or round the neck and pulled up over the back of the head, covering the ears, like a Balaclava helmet.

## Übermantel
Surcoat

This garment, introduced as early as 1937, was a long, loose fitting and heavily lined version of the greatcoat, designed to be worn over the ordinary greatcoat, or sheepskin or fur waistcoat by drivers of open motor vehicles. Early models had black and aluminium twisted cord around the collar, the same colour as the coat, and the national emblem on the left sleeve. Basic cut was identical to that of the greatcoat.

During the war many different patterns of this coat were issued, and in addition to the normal side pockets they were equipped with two vertical pockets above the waist, which were so placed and sufficiently large to conveniently take a gloved or mittened hand. The surcoat was lined with dark grey blanketing or brown fur; some had field-grey leather patches on the shoulders.

*The term 'special winter clothing' (Winter-Sonderbekleidung) was reserved for the special winter combat clothing suitable for wear in action, as opposed to other types of winter clothing worn by personnel behind the front.

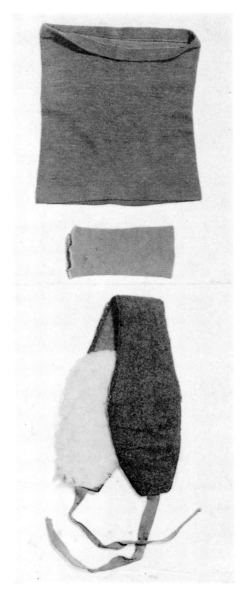

Issue field-grey knitted woollen toque (Kopfschützer) and wrist warmers. Typical ear-defenders made from field-grey cloth lined with lamb's wool. It covered the ears and was tied under the chin.

Surcoat, obverse and reverse and detail of raised hood.

## Wachmantel

Guard coat

This was a traditional garment (surcoat) for sentries on static guard duty in extreme cold. It was usually made of sheepskin and worn together with straw over boots.

In January 1943 Pohl reported that 'thanks to supplies obtained in the Balkans, and by the change of domicile of the Jews, the Waffen-SS was able to obtain sufficient stocks, and was able also this year to line anoraks with fur. Next year, however, we must also change over to the winter clothing introduced in the army'. [4]

Following a crash programme, the army succeeded in issuing its new winter combat uniform to field units in time for the winter of 1942–3, but apart from odd sets obtained from the army by the Waffen-SS, its own version of this clothing did not enter service until the winter of 1943–4. The clothing consisted of a hood, jacket, trousers, and mittens, made from two layers of wind proof material, with wool–rayon interlining. It was reversible, being white on one side and SS autumn camouflage on the other, and was designed either to be worn over the ordinary field uniform or in conjunction with special quilted under garments. The white side of this uniform tended to get filthy, which defeated its purpose as camouflage in a snowy landscape, so troops behind the front were ordered to wear it with the camouflage side out.

## Recognition

Because of basic similarity in shape (or shapelessness) and colour of winter clothing, a system of markings had to be introduced to identify one side from the other. On the Russian front a strip of black cloth was worn on the upper left or right arm, and changed daily, so that it could not be imitated by the enemy; the 1943 pattern winter combat jacket was provided with buttons on the sleeves, so that the strip could easily be changed. Waffen-SS personnel also wore the death's head on the front of the fur cap, sometimes accompanied by the national emblem.

## Notes:

1. V.Bl.d.W.-SS., Nr.14, 1 December 1940, Ziff.419.
2. Ibid., Nr.8, 15 April 1942, Ziff.136.
3. Ibid., Nr.18, 15 September 1942, Ziff. 330.
4. SS-Ogruf.u.Gen.d.W.-SS Oswald Pohl an den RF-SS, Betr:Bericht Über die Rohstofflage auf dem Spinnstoff-und Ledergebiet. Berlin, den 9 January 1943.

SS-Gruf. u. Gen.Lt. d. W.-SS Felix Steiner wearing an issue surcoat with leather shoulder pads. The SS-Oscha. wears the standard field-grey greatcoat.

The 1942 SS winter combat uniform. The soldier on the right wears a toque.

Group of SS grenadiers in 1944, wearing the new pattern field cap, while one wears a captured Soviet winter cap with SS insignia. Some of the men wear the SS version of the special army winter combat uniform.

SS reversible winter combat uniform consisting of jacket, trousers, hood and mittens, introduced in 1943.

## TROPENBEKLEIDUNG

Tropical clothing
Tropical clothing came rather late to the Waffen-SS*, and is believed to have been first issued to members of the Sturmbrigade Reichsführer-SS on their arrival on Corsica in September 1943. Although there was talk of sending the Waffen-SS to north Africa, the clothing was designed primarily for wear in southern Europe, the Balkans, Adriatic, and southern Russia, and consisted of the following items:
1. Sun helmet
2. Field cap (Schiffchen)
3. Standard field cap
4. Field blouse
5. Shirt
6. Field trousers
7. Shorts

All the above items were basically the same in cut and manufacture as their field-grey counterparts, but all were made out of a sand coloured cotton drill.

### Tropenhelm

Tropical helmet
The shape was the same as that issued to German troops in North Africa, and was made of cork covered with olive green cotton drill. All external leather trimming was in field-grey, and the helmet had a red lining. The SS runes and national colours were the same as those worn on the steel helmet, but were detachable white metal shields.[1]

### Feldmütze (Schiffchen)

Field cap
Identical in cut to the new pattern field-grey field cap. (See p. 73.)

### Einheitsfeldmütze

Standard field cap
The same shape as its field-grey counterpart, but without separate flap and buttons in front. The same insignia was worn on both caps, and consisted of a national emblem and death's head, machine-woven in sand coloured artificial silk thread on a black ground.

* The first mention of tropical clothing in the SS-Verordnungsblatt is in Nr.19, 1 October 1943, Ziff.370.

Improvised tropical clothing in Greece 1941, consisting of sports clothes and captured British sun helmets.

SS-Obersturmbannführer Gesele, commander of the Sturmbrigade Reichsführer-SS, soon after his unit had been issued with tropical clothing, Corsica, September 1943.

## Feldbluse
Field blouse

There were two basic patterns of tropical field blouse, as well as a number of minor variants. The first was identical in cut to the 1940 model army field blouse, the second was based on the very efficient Italian bush jacket (Sahariana).

Normally only badges of rank and the national emblem were worn on the tropical field blouse, although other insignia, such as collar patches and nationality badges, were also worn by individuals.[2] The national emblem was machine-woven in sand coloured artificial silk on a black ground, and N.C.O.s lace, which appeared on the collar and sleeve chevrons was also woven in sand coloured artificial silk.

## Hemd
Shirt

The shirt was also manufactured in the same way as the Italian Sahariana, with two breast patch pockets.

## Feldhose
Field trousers

These were in the standard trouser cut, with built-in cloth belt, two slanting side pockets with flaps and buttons, watch pocket, and hip pocket with button. The bottom of the trouser leg tapered and was fastened around the ankle with a draw-string and footstrap.

## Kurzhose
Shorts

Possibly not official issue, but certainly worn by certain Waffen-SS personnel. Same cloth belt and pocket arrangement as the field trousers.

## Notes:

1. This is a description of the helmet illustrated (only surviving example known at time of writing) from the collection of Mr James van Fleet, Stanhope, New Jersey, U.S.A.
2. See the Waffen-SS. Its Divisional Insignia., p. 63, with illustration.

SS tropical helmet.

Two Romanian Volksdeutsche in the Wiking Division, wearing tropical uniform and mountain boots.

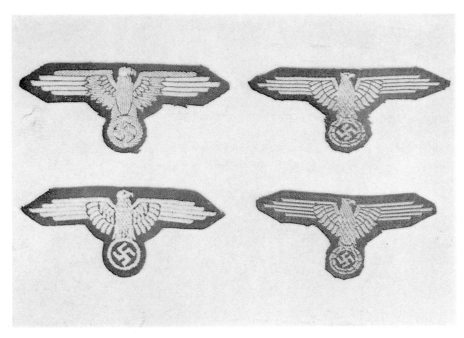

National emblems for wear on the sleeve, L-R: hand embroidered and machine woven pattern for officers. Bottom row, L-R: machine embroidered and machine woven pattern for other ranks.

## ÄRMELHOHEITSABZEICHEN

National emblem for the sleeve

The national emblem first began to be worn on the upper left sleeve of the earth-grey SS uniform in the summer of 1935. Contrary to popular belief, it was not generally worn by all ranks on the field-grey tunic, blouse, and greatcoat until 1938. Prior to that year officers usually wore a hand-embroidered version, other ranks a machine-embroidered version if the field blouse or greatcoat had been issued with it on.

In 1938 the second and final pattern of the SS national emblem in aluminium hand embroidery for officers, and machine embroidered in silver grey silk thread for other ranks, began to be generally issued, and were listed in the SS price list issued by the RZM.[1] Photographic evidence suggests, however, that the original pattern was still in use in November 1938.[2] In 1939 the national emblem began to be woven in aluminium thread for officers and silver grey thread for other ranks. This pattern was to remain in use until the end of the war.

A common habit (open to a number of interpretations) was the wearing by Waffen-SS officers of national emblems other than that of the SS on both the head-dress and sleeve. Most common were those of the army, although national emblems of the NSDAP were also worn. This practice, which was of course, unofficial, was most common between 1939–40, when the SS-VT became the Waffen-SS.

During this period of rapid expansion, SS insignia for the field-grey uniform were still controlled by the RZM, who gave priority to clothing depots, so that RZM outlets had difficulty in obtaining stocks. Army insignia on the other hand were in plentiful supply and available, over the counter, in military outfitters throughout the country. The appearance of army national emblems on SS uniforms later in the war was due to the fact that those who had earlier purchased army emblems continued to wear them, and army insignia remained easier to obtain at the front and in occupied territories than that of the SS.

Throughout the war the national emblem continued to be worn on the upper left arm of nearly all Waffen-SS uniforms and clothing (in cloth, cotton drill, and camouflage material) although officially it was not to be worn on camouflage clothing.[4]

The wartime pattern was in fact the woven type, manufactured in aluminium thread for officers and silver grey silk for other ranks. The shade of the thread used for the national emblems of other ranks varied considerably including white, matt-grey, and beige, added to which fading and dirt tended to alter the colours. However, the following different coloured threads were used for specific types of uniform:

Aluminium wire on black ground for officers.

Silver grey thread on black ground for other ranks.

Light khaki (sand coloured) thread on black ground for wear on tropical uniforms.

Brown on black ground for camouflage uniforms (autumn). [5]

Bright green on black ground for camouflage uniforms (spring). [5]

## HOHEITSABZEICHEN FÜR KOPFBEDECKNUNG

National emblem for head-dress

At first the SA and SS shared the same small white metal (tin) national emblem, which was worn on front of the service cap, above the SA button, or SS death's head. In the summer of 1935 the Leibstandarte-SS Adolf Hitler was equipped with earth-grey, and a photograph of seven officers in brand new earth-grey uniforms shows two wearing the Reichswehr national emblem on their service caps. It may be assumed that this was just another case of 'Eigenmächtigkeit' (personal vanity), or that certain LAH officers wished to emphasise their military standing by wearing army as opposed to political insignia. In February 1936 Hitler inspected and approved a new SS version of the national emblem for the service cap. The badge was made of silvered Lupal (synthetic alloy) for the black extra cap, and matt aluminium for the black, earth-grey or field-grey service cap.[6]

This national emblem remained in use until the end of the war as the standard pattern metal SS national emblem, although both types of metal and finish used varied considerably. Hand-embroidered versions of the SS national emblem were very rare, and most of those in private collections were made after the war for use in theatrical productions. Certain officers wore either the hand-embroidered or woven army national emblem on their field service caps, while others wore the SS sleeve version, but none of these unofficial modes had any significance whatsoever.

**Notes:**

1. SS-Preisliste Nr.3, 1 January 1938.
2. See photograph on p. 18
3. SS-Preisliste Nr.4, March 1939.
4. See orders quoted in section on camouflage clothing.
5. See source of this information in footnotes to section dealing with camouflage clothing.
6. Adjutant des Führers, Hptm.a.D.Wiedermann An die Reichsführung-SS.Betr.Hoheitsabzeichen für die SS-Mütze, Berlin, den 3 February 1936.

Top to bottom L-R: Badges for the old and new pattern field cap. Combined badge for the standard field cap, machine embroidered and machine woven patterns for wear on field grey head-dress. Machine embroidered and machine woven patterns for wear on black head-dress.

Standard metal cap insignia.

## TOTENKOPFABZEICHEN (STOFF)

Death's head badges (cloth)

The first cloth version of the death's head badge was not made for the SS Panzer beret.

In 1939, SS death's heads began to be machine woven in aluminium thread for the new pattern SS officers' field cap.[1] With the introduction, in November 1940, of the new style SS field cap, the death's head began to be machine woven in silver grey silk thread for other ranks, in addition to the pattern in aluminium thread. This pattern was manufactured until late in the war, when it began to be replaced by the new combined death's head and national emblem for wear on the M.1943 standard field cap.[2] The machine woven death's head was manufactured in a standard size for wear on all the various kinds of field cap, and was even worn by some personnel on the service cap. A slightly larger version was, however, produced for wear on the Fez. (See Vol. 7; section on the 13th SS Div.) The same colour threads were used for the manufacture of death's heads as were used for national emblems.

## TOTENKOPFABZEICHEN FÜR DIENSTMÜTZE

Death's head cap badge

The death's head was worn on nearly all items of SS head-dress beneath the national emblem. The death's head was adopted by Hitler's Stosstrupp in 1923, and was to remain the symbol of the SS until the end of the war. The first pattern was identical to that worn by the Prussian Life Hussar Regiment Nos. 1 and 2, and was made of silvered tin. In 1934 it was replaced by a specially designed SS model. Both old and new badges were worn concurrently, but by the outbreak of war only a few Waffen-SS officers continued to wear the old pattern.[3]

Like the national emblem, the death's head was manufactured first in silvered tin, and then in an alloy. The death's head for wear on the grey service cap was to be in matt aluminium, and silver plated for the black walking-out cap. Although intended for wear only on the service cap and the N.C.O.s field cap, the metal death's head was worn on other types of head-dress such as the field cap, standard field and ski cap, and on various kinds of fur cap.[4]

### Notes:

1. SS-Preisliste, Nr.4, April 1939, with hand-written amendments.
2. See section on head-dress.
3. See illustration on p. 58.
4. See illustration on p. 70.

## SS-DIENSTGRADE (ACTIV)
SS Regular ranks

| **I. SS-Männer (Men)** **(non-SS members)** | **1938-1941** **(SS-Members)** | **1941-45** |
|---|---|---|
| 1. SS-Bewerber | | |
| 2. Staffel-Anwärter | SS-Anwärter | SS-Schütze u.s.w. |
| 3. Staffel-Mann | SS-Mann | SS-Oberschütze u.s.w. |
| 4. Staffel-Sturmmann | SS-Sturmmann | SS-Sturmmann |
| 5. | SS-Rottenführer | SS-Rottenführer |
| 6. | | SS-Rottenführer (2. Gehaltsstufe) |
| **IIa. SS-Unterführer ohne Portepee (Junior N.C.O.s)** | | |
| 7. | SS-Unterscharführer | SS-Unterscharführer |
| 8. | SS-Scharführer | SS-Scharführer |
| **IIb. SS-Unterführer mit Portepee (Senior N.C.O.s/Warrant officers)** | | |
| 9. | SS-Oberscharführer | SS-Oberscharführer |
| 10. | SS-Hauptscharführer | SS-Hauptscharführer |
| 11. | SS-Sturmscharführer | SS-Sturmscharführer |
| **IIIa. SS-Führer (Company officers)** | | |
| 12. | SS-Untersturmführer | SS-Untersturmführer |
| 13. | SS-Obersturmführer | SS-Obersturmführer |
| 14. | SS-Hauptsturmführer | SS-Hauptsturmführer |
| **IIIb. SS-Führer (Field officers)** | | |
| 15. | SS-Sturmbannführer | SS-Sturmbannführer |
| 16. | SS-Obersturmbannführer | SS-Obersturmbannführer |
| 17. | SS-Standartenführer | SS-Standartenführer |
| 18. | SS-Oberführer | SS-Oberführer |
| **IV. Höhere SS-Führer (General officers)** | | |
| 19. | SS-Brigadeführer | SS-Brigaf.u.Gen.Maj.d.W.-SS u.s.w. |
| 20. | SS-Gruppenführer | SS-Gruf.u.Gen.Lt.d.W.-SS u.s.w. |
| 21. | SS-Obergruppenführer | SS-Ogruf.u.Gen.d.W.-SS u.s.w. |
| 22. | | SS-Oberst-Gruppenführer u. Gen.Obst.d.W.-SS*. |

*Introduced on 7 April 1942.

## Explanatory guide to regular rank listing

**I.**

1. A suitable member of the Hitler Youth who wanted to join the SS, became an SS-Bewerber at the age of eighteen. On the Reich Party Day of the same year he was accepted as a Staffel-Anwärter.[1]

2. SS-Anwärter was the collective designation for all SS men during their first three years of service, and who, according to Order No.A/9434 of 9 November 1935, had not yet been accepted as full SS members. With effect from 1 June 1936 the rank designations for SS-Anwärter were:[2]
   Staffel-Anwärter
   Staffel-Mann
   Staffel-Sturmmann etc.

3. SS-Mann was the collective designation for all fully entitled SS members up to and including the Reichsführer-SS, who had been finally accepted in the SS, or who were still to be finally accepted. The rank designations for SS men were:[3]
   SS-Sturmmann
   SS-Rottenführer etc.

In 1941 the traditional party ranks of SS-Anwärter and SS-Mann were changed to the army ranks of Schütze and Oberschütze.[4] These ranks varied according to the type of unit in which the holder served. By March 1943 the following titles were in use in the Waffen-SS.[5]

| | | |
|---|---|---|
| SS-Panzer-Rgt. | SS-Panzerschütze | SS-Panzeroberschütze |
| SS-Pz.-Gren.-Rgt. | SS-Panzergrenadier | SS-Pz.-Obergrenadier |
| SS-Gren.-Rgt. | SS-Grenadier | SS-Obergrenadier |
| SS-Geb.-Jäger-Rgt. | SS-Jäger | SS-Oberschütze* |
| SS-Reiter-Rgt. | SS-Reiter | SS-Oberreiter |
| SS-Art.-Rgt. | SS-Kanonier | SS-Oberkanonier |
| SS-Geb.-Art.-Rgt. | SS-Kanonier | SS-Oberkanonier |
| SS-Sturmgesch.-Einh. | SS-Kanonier | SS-Oberkanonier |
| SS-Panzer-Jäg.-Einh. | SS-Schütze | SS-Oberschütze |
| SS-Kradsch.-Einh. | SS-Schütze | SS-Oberschütze |
| SS-Panzer-Späh-Einh. | SS-Panzerschütze | SS-Panzeroberschütze |
| SS-Flak-Einh. | SS-Kanonier | SS-Oberkanonier |
| SS-Pionier-Einh. | SS-Pionier | SS-Oberpionier |

*In this particular case there was no change to avoid confusion with the traditional mountain and paratroop rank Oberjäger which corresponded to Unteroffizier.

| | | |
|---|---|---|
| SS-Nachr.-Einh. | SS-Funker | SS-Oberfunker |
| SS-Werfer-Einh. | SS-Kanonier | SS-Oberkanonier |
| SS-Radfahr-Einh. | SS-Schütze | SS-Oberschütze |
| SS-Nachschub-Einh. (besp.) | SS-Fahrer | SS-Oberfahrer |
| SS-Nachschub-Einh. (mot) | SS-Kraftfahrer | SS-Oberkraftfahrer |
| SS-Sanitäts-Einh. | SS-Schütze | SS-Oberschütze |
| SS-Veterinär-Einh. | SS-Reiter | SS-Oberreiter |
| SS-Werkstatt-Einh. | SS-Schütze | SS-Oberschütze |
| SS-Feldgend.-Einh. | SS-Feldgendarm | |
| SS-Karstwehr-Btl. | SS-Jäger | SS-Oberschütze |
| SS-Wehrgeologen-Btl. | SS-Schütze | SS-Oberschütze |
| SS-Kriegsbericht.Abt. | SS-Schütze | SS-Oberschütze |
| SS-Bewährungs-Einh. | SS-Bewährungs-schütze | SS-Bewährungs-Oberschütze[6] |

Promotion to SS-Oberschütze u.s.w. took place after at least six months service in the field or replacement army. The wearing of the Oberschützen star (on the left sleeve) by SS men with only six weeks or three months service was not authorised.[7]

4 & 5. The rank titles SS-Sturmmann and SS-Rottenführer remained unchanged irrespective of the type of unit.

6. In January 1942 the army re-introduced a new rank, Stabsgefreiter neuer Art, but it was decided not to follow suit in the Waffen-SS. Instead an SS-Rottenführer with at least five years service (including two months in the field) or six years service could be proposed for promotion by their battalion commander to a newly introduced pay grade SS-Rottenführer (2. Gehaltsstufe) which corresponded to the new army rank.[8]

SS-FHA/Kdo.W.-SS/IIb/IV.

**II.**

**SS-Unterführer.** Any suitable SS man irrespective of rank could be appointed SS-Stabsscharführer by his unit after a three year probationary period. After a further three months, and on the application of his commander, he was entitled to wear an aluminium chevron on the lower right sleeve. On relinquishing this office the chevron was to be removed.[9] During the war N.C.O.s with the rank of SS-Hauptscharführer and SS-Sturmscharführer could be appointed SS-Stabsscharführer and could wear two rows of N.C.O.s lace, 0.5 cm apart and approximately 13 cm from the bottom of the sleeve, and above the cuff band. N.C.O.s with the rank of

SS-Unterscharführer up to and including SS-Oberscharführer holding this appointment could also wear the lace on the cuff and were known as SS-Stabsscharführerdiensttuer (acting Stabsscharführer). See page 20.

11. Introduced on the 23 January 1938 to correspond to the army rank of Stabsfeldwebel. Senior N.C.O.s at the beginning of their thirteenth year of service were eligible for promotion by the Inspekteur der SS-Verfügungstruppe.[10]

III.
18. SS-Oberführer was the only SS rank which did not have an army equivalent, but which was in fact a senior Colonel. He was entitled to wear the silver grey lapels and aluminium cap piping of a general officer, but only the shoulder straps of an SS-Standartenführer.

IV.
20. On 14 November 1939 the first two SS divisional commanders, SS-Gruppenführer Paul Hausser and Theodor Eicke were given the appointment and badges of rank (shoulder straps) of a Generalleutnant.[11]

19-21. During the course of 1940 all Waffen-SS general officers were given corresponding army titles:[12]
   SS-Brigadeführer und Generalmajor der Waffen-SS
   SS-Gruppenführer und Generalleutnant der Waffen-SS
   SS-Obergruppenführer und General der Waffen-SS
In 1943 general officers in the police (Ordnungspolizei) who had commanded Waffen-SS formations in the field were given corresponding Waffen-SS ranks:[13]
   SS-Obergruppenführer und General der Polizei und der Waffen-SS
On the 1 July 1944 seventeen senior SS and police leaders (Höhere-SS und Polizeiführer) were taken into the Waffen-SS and awarded the designation:[14]
   SS-Obergruppenführer und General der Polizei und der Waffen-SS

22. On 7 April 1942 Hitler approved the introduction of a new SS rank, SS-Oberstgruppenführer.[15] The first promotion to this rank was dated 20 April 1942, when the commander of the LSSAH, Joseph 'Sepp' Dietrich, became the first SS-Oberstgruppenführer und Panzer General-oberst der Waffen-SS.* For some reason he was not actually informed

*At first this new rank was written as one word, but in order to avoid confusion with the rank SS-Obergruppenführer it was ordered to be written with a hyphen.[16]

of his promotion, and did not begin to wear the badges of rank of an SS-Oberst-Gruppenführer until 23 August 1944. Panzer-Generaloberst der Waffen-SS was an honorary title to commemorate his service in the embryo tank arm during the First World War. On 1 August 1944 the Commander-in-Chief of the 7th Army, Paul Hausser, was promoted SS-Oberst-Gruppenführer and Generaloberst der Waffen-SS. This was the second and possibly last promotion to this rank in the Waffen-SS.[17]

## Qualification

During the course of the war there was an enormous increase in the number of SS men with special qualifications in various different careers (Sonderlaufbahnen). On completion of their training they were authorised to add an abbreviated form of their career to their rank title as follows:

## Notes:

1. Die SS., pp. 18-19.
2. Der Reichsführer-SS, Der Chef des SS-Hauptamtes Z.K.Tgb.Nr. Ch.1003/36.,Betr.:Dienstgradabzeichen in der SS., Bezug.: Befehl RFSS Tgb.A/9434, 9 November 1935, Berlin, den 25 May 1936.
3. Ibid.
4. V.Bl.d.W.-SS., Nr.14, 15 July 1941.
5. V.Bl.d.W.-SS., Nr.5, 1 March 1943, Ziff.94.
6. Sonderanhang zum V.Bl.d.W.-SS., Nr.21, 1 November 1944, Ziff.110.
7. Ibid., Nr.  .
8. Ibid., Nr.17, 1 September 1942, Ziff.317.
9. Der Chef des SS-Hauptamtes IA/C Az.B. 23d/11.2.38., Betr.: Winkel für Stabsscharführer., Bezug.: RFSS Az.R 23 d/18 June 1937, Berlin, den 11 February 1938.
10.
11. Die Waffen-SS eine Dokumentation., pp. 489-94.
12. Ibid.
13. Ibid.
14. Ibid.
15. Ibid.
16. V.Bl.d.W.-SS., Nr.13, 15 June 1942, Ziff.192.
17. The Dienstalterliste der SS der NSDAP, Stand vom 30 Januar 1944, lists two SS-Oberst-Gruppenführer, neither of whom were members of the Waffen-SS. Dietrich is listed as an SS-Obergruppenführer u.Kom.Gen.I.SS.-Pz.Korps.

| Career Officers | Abbreviation | Example |
|---|---|---|
| 1. Doctor, Dentist, Chemist | San. | SS-Untersturmführer (San.) |
| 2. Veterinary Surgeon | Vet. | SS-Obersturmführer (Vet.) |
| 3. Specialist | S | SS-Sturmbannführer (S) |
| then | F | SS-Sturmbannführer (F) |

**N.C.O.s**

| | | |
|---|---|---|
| 4. Vet. | Vet. | SS-Oberscharführer (Vet.) |
| 5. Technical Quarter Master Sergeant | Schirrm.K, F or P etc. | SS-Oberscharführer (Schirrm.P) |
| 6. Farrier | Hufbeschl. | SS-Unterscharführer (Hufbeschl.) |
| 7. Artificer | Feuerw. | SS-Oberscharführer (Feuerw.) |
| 8. Technical N.C.O. | TUFW | SS-Hauptscharführer (TUFW). |
| 9. Foreman of signals | Fkmst. | SS-Hauptscharführer (Fkmst.) |
| 10. Musician* | Mus. | SS-Oberscharführer (Mus.) |
| 11. Cook* | Koch | SS-Unterscharführer (Koch) |
| 12. Medical Orderly* | San. | SS-Unterscharführer (San.) |

*Also for other ranks.

## Character

The expansion of the Waffen-SS and the acceptance in its ranks of those, who, according to fundamental SS racist principles could not be accepted as full members of the SS, brought about the development of SS rank titles to include the character of Waffen-SS personnel. Non-German nationals from Germanic countries serving in legions were to replace the prefix SS by Legion or Leg., i.e. Leg.-Schütze or Legion.-Sturmbannführer. To identify personnel serving in units of the Waffen-SS recruited from neither German nationals nor Germanic countries, the prefix Waffen was added both to the formation designation, i.e., 13. Waffen-Gebirgs-Division der SS Handschar (kroatische Nr.1), and the rank, i.e., Waffen-Untersturmführer der SS etc.

## Notes:

1. V.Bl.d.W.-SS., Nr.16, 15 March 1943, Ziff.112.
3. Der Reichsführer-SS, SS-Befehl., Betr.:Fachführer und Fachunterführer der Waffen-SS., Abschrift, Berlin, den 21 June 1942.
7. Ibid., Nr.22, 15 November 1943, Ziff.449.
8. Prior to the 1 November 1944 the designation was Unterführer im Waffentechn.Dienst, i.e. SS-Unterscharführer (UiwD).

## Führernachwuchs

Officer cadets

With the official opening of the first SS officers' school in Bad Tölz on 1 October 1934 four new ranks for officer cadets were introduced.[1]

### C. Führernachwuchs

SS-Führeranwärter
SS-Standartenjunker
SS-Fähnrich (SS-Scharführer)
SS-Oberfähnrich (SS-Hauptscharführer)

SS-Führeranwärter are those SS men who have been assembled on orders of the Reichsführung-SS for later training at SS-Schule Tölz.

SS-Standartenjunker are those SS men undergoing training at Führerschule Tölz.

Promotion to SS-Fähnrich is by order of the Führerschule Tölz, following the successful completion of the RF-SS examination, and on the recommendation of the school commander.

Promotion to SS-Oberfähnrich follows the successful completion of the final examination at the Führerschule Tölz, and on the recommendation of the Commander of Führerschule Tölz to the RF-SS.

Further regulations concerning the above will be issued by the Chief of Abt.P I.

Der Reichsführer-SS
H. Himmler

In March 1935 the titles of SS officer cadets were altered.

## Nr.16: Organisation and ranks in the SS.[2]

Ziffer 5 C, Führernachwuchs, of the SS-Befehls-Blatt, 15 October 1934, No. 10, is hereby amended:

### C. Führernachwuchs

SS-Führeranwärter
SS-Junker
SS-Standartenjunker (SS-Scharführer)
SS-Standartenoberjunker (SS-Hauptscharführer)

SS-Führeranwärter are those SS men assembled by the Reichsführung-SS for later training at SS schools in Tölz and Braunschweig.

SS-Junker are those SS men undergoing training at SS schools in Tölz or Braunschweig.

Promotion to SS-Standartenjunker follows the successful completion of the preliminary examination of the Reichsführer-SS, and on the recommendation of the school commander.

Promotion to SS-Standartenoberjunker follows the successful completion of the final examination and on the recommendation of the school commander to the Reichsführer-SS.

SS-Führeranwärter, etc. wear the badges of their rank and the insignia of their former unit.

SS-Hauptamt, Führungsamt

## Führerbewerber
Potential officers

In December 1940 the Reichsführer-SS approved the introduction of the designation Potential officer (SS-Führerbewerber) in order to prevent valuable human material from being pushed into the background, and thus lost in units, if they were considered to be suitable to succeed the present Waffen-SS officers. The following categories of persons were to be recruited as potential officers, and promoted (depending of course on ability) as quickly as possible to Führeranwärter and officer or reserve officer of the Waffen-SS:

Members of NAPOLA*
Political leaders
Hitler Youth leaders with the rank of Bannführer and above.
Those with matriculation (Abiturienten)

The designation Führerbewerber was to be entered in the personal documents of those accepted as such, and the SS-Personalhauptamt was to be notified (via the Kommando der Waffen-SS), so that it could pursue their promotion.[3] In March 1942 it was decided to hold special courses for SS-Führerbewerber z.V. (zur Verfügung) who, because of injuries sustained in the field, could no longer participate in the courses for SS-Junker or Reserve-Führer-Anwärter (SS-Junker-resp. Reserve-Führer-Anwärter-Lehrgänge). On completion of the course the SS-Bewerber z.V. would be promoted to SS-Oberscharführer der Reserve, and after satisfactory service in one of the SS offices, he could be promoted to SS-Untersturmführer d.Res.z.V. etc.[4] The same order increased the sphere of those members of the Waffen-SS who were to be considered as potential officers:

Leaders of the Allgemeine-SS
Hitler Youth leaders with the rank of Stammführer and above.
Political leaders (Hoheitsträger der Partei)
Those with matriculation.
Graduates of NAPOLA

*National Political Training Establishments.

Leaders of the Reich Labour Corps with the rank of Feldmeister and above
Staff and cadets of the Ordensburgen of the NSDAP
Leaders of other Party organisations.

The outbreak of the war, and the rapid expansion of the Waffen-SS, saw the intake of those who only intended to serve in the Waffen-SS for the duration of the war. Instead of becoming regular (Activ), they became reserve officers (Führer der Reserve), after undergoing special Reserve Officer Candidate course at an officers' school.[5]

## Regular [6]
Führerbewerber (FB) was an untrained potential officer on commencement of four months basic training (Vorbereitungslehrgang).

SS-Junker (equivalent in rank to an SS-Unterscharführer) was an SS-Führeranwärter (FA) who, having completed four months with a basic training unit, underwent a six-month course (Kriegs-Junker-Lehrgang) at an officers' school, during which he was required to pass an intermediate exmination. On passing he was appointed SS-Standartenjunker.

SS-Standartenjunker (SS-Scharführer) was an SS-Junker who had passed the intermediate examination while at officers' school.

SS-Standartenoberjunker (SS-Hauptscharführer) was an SS-Standartenjunker who had successfully completed the six-month course at officers' school, passed the final examination, and accepted by the Chief of the Department for Officer Training (Chef des Amtes für Führerausbildung – Amt XI im SS-FHA). As a graduate officer cadet, the SS-Standartenoberjunker was sent back to his unit, where after a minimum period of two months he received promotion to SS-Untersturmführer, etc.

## Reserve (des Beurlaubtenstandes) [7]
Reserve-Führer-Bewerber (RFB) attended a four months Reserve-Führer-Anwärter-Lehrgang in the troop or administrative service, and on successful completion was appointed Reserve-Führer-Anwärter (RFA) and promoted to the rank of SS-Oberscharführer d.Res.* He was then returned to his unit, where after a minimum period of two months he received promotion to SS-Untersturmführer d.Res., etc.**

*It was not necessary for an SS-Oscha. or SS-Hscha. to have been a Reserve-Führer-Anwärter, since he could have been an ordinary N.C.O., but if he had it was thought that he was to use the letters RFA or RFB after his rank title.

**This rank could also be attained by bravery in the field.

## Waffen-SS Potential Regular officers (Führerbewerber) 1943

| | | | |
|---|---|---|---|
| SS-Schütze usw. (FB) | SS-Schütze usw. (FB) | SS-Schütze usw. (FB) | SS-Schütze usw. |
| SS-Sturmmann (FA) | SS-Sturmmann (FA) | | SS-Sturmmann |
| SS-Junker | SS-Junker | | SS-Unterscharführer |
| | SS-Standartenjunker | | |
| | | SS-Oberscharführer (FA) | SS-Oberscharführer |
| SS-Standartenoberjunker | SS-Standartenoberjunker | | SS-Hauptscharführer |
| became | | | |

| | | | |
|---|---|---|---|
| SS-Untersturmführer | SS-Untersturmführer | SS-Untersturmführer or | SS-Untersturmführer |
| | | SS-Obersturmführer or | |
| | | SS-Hauptsturmführer | |

## Career (Laufbahn)

| | | | | | | | |
|---|---|---|---|---|---|---|---|
| Ia-e | (Truppendienst) | IVa | (Technischer Führer K I) | VIIc | (Arzt)* | V | (Techn. SS-Führer (W))*** |
| II | (Verwaltungsdienst) | IVc | (Technischer Führer K II) | IXc | (Zahnarzt) | XVI | (Musikführer)** |
| III | (Waffen-u.Mun.Dienst)*** | | | XIa | (Veterinär) | | |
| VIIa | (Arzt) | | | | | | |
| IXa | (Zahnarzt) | | | | | | |
| Xa | (Apotheker) | | | | | | |
| XIb | (Veterinär) | | | | | | |
| XIIa | (Richter) | | | | | | |
| XIV | (Sipo u.SD) | | | | | | |
| XVa | (Wehrgeologe) | | | | | | |

## General Note:

Laufbahn V (Technischer Führer W u.W(Ing.)) were commissioned on completing the N.C.O. Career Course U 16 (Techn. Unterführer) with the rank of SS-Hauptscharführer.

*Already qualified (mit Studium) before entering service either as regular or reserve officers.

**No FB or FA had officer training on becoming SS-Untersturmführer.

***In 1945, Laufbahn III was amalgamated with Laufbahn V (Techn. Führer (W)) in the new Laufbahn SS-Führer des Feldzeugdienstes.

## Waffen-SS Potential Reserve Officers (Führerbewerber der Beurlaubtenstandes (RFB))

| | | |
|---|---|---|
| SS-Schütze usw. (RFB) | SS-Schütze usw. (RFB) | SS-Schütze usw. (RFB) |
| SS-Sturmmann (RFA) | | SS-Sturmmann (RFA) |
| SS-Unterscharführer (RFA) | | SS-Unterscharführer (RFA) |
| SS-Oberscharführer (RFA) | SS-Oberscharführer (RFA) | SS-Oberscharführer (RFA) |
| | SS-Hauptscharführer (RFA) | SS-Hauptscharführer (RFA) |

became

SS-Untersturmführer d.B.          SS-Untersturmführer d.B.          SS-Untersturmführer d.B.

## Career (Laufbahn)

| | | |
|---|---|---|
| Ia-e (Truppendienst d.B.) | VIIb (Arzt d.B.) | XId (Veterinär d.R.) **** |
| II (Verwaltungsdienst d.B.) | IXb (Zahnarzt d.B.) | |
| IVb (Techn. Führer K I d.B.) | Xb (Apotheker d.R.) | |
| IVd (Techn. Führer K II d.B.) | XIc (Veterinär d.R.) | |
| VI (Techn. Führer N) | | |
| VIII (San. Techn. Dienst) | | |
| XIIb (Richter d.B.) | | |
| XIII (Beurkundungsführer) * | | |
| XVb (Wehrgeologe) * | | |
| XVc (Wehrgeologe) ** | | |
| XVd (Wehrgeologe) *** | | |

  *Became a regular.

 **Already qualified.

***Already qualified in other branches.

****Usually only students.

In February 1944 the somewhat complicated system of titles and ranks was simplified in order to ensure uniform planning and integration of potential officers in the Waffen-SS.[8] With the approval of the Reichsführer-SS, the following it was ordered that as from the 1 February 1944 all SS-Führer-bewerber will be promoted to

SS-Standartenoberjunker or
SS-Standartenoberjunker der Reserve or
SS-Frw. Standartenoberjunker ;*

before being proposed for promotion to :
SS-Untersturmführer
SS-Untersturmführer der Reserve or
SS-Frw. Untersturmführer

This particularly applied to exceptional cases in which promotion to SS-Untersturmführer took place without attendance at a course, or due to the granting of a corresponding Waffen-SS rank to Germanic volunteer potential officers (germ. Frw. Führerbewerber) or former officers of foreign armies.**
As before promotion to SS-Standartenoberjunker, etc., was pronounced by the Chief of Amt XI in the SS-FHA. SS-Standartenoberjunker who had not attended a course were to apply via their units for promotion to SS-Ustuf., after at least two months trial, to the SS-Personalhauptamt via the SS-FHA.Amt V Abt.11a. This also applied in cases of special achievement, such as bravery, etc.
As from 1 February 1944 the designation Reserve-Führer-Anwärter der Waffen-SS (RFA) was abolished, and in its place the following were introduced :

SS-Junker der Reserve
SS-Standartenjunker der Reserve
SS-Standartenoberjunker der Reserve

*In this context Frw. or Freiwilligen literally means that the person in question was a volunteer from a Germanic country. It was not an official prefix. See page 80.

**Officers of the German army, Reichswehr, Imperial Austro-Hungarian army were commissioned directly into the Waffen-SS, and in exceptional cases so were some foreigners.

All existing Reserve-Führer-Anwärter der Waffen-SS (RFA) appointed by SS-FHA Amt XI will, as from 1 February 1944 be re-designated and promoted to SS-Standartenoberjunker d.Res. This also applied to all SS-Unterführer d.Res and Reserve-Führer-Bewerber before being proposed for promotion to SS-Ustuf.d.Res.

**Notes :**

1. SS-Befehls-Blatt., Nr.10, 15 October 1934, Nr.5.
2. Ibid., Nr.3, 25 March 1935, Nr.16.
3. SS-FHA (az. 17/2 December 1940/jü/Pc.) Einführung der Bezeichnung Führerbewerber als SS-Führer-Bewerber z.V., Berlin den 5 March 1942.
5. Reserve officers were introduced in the Waffen-SS in December 1939, see section on shoulder straps.
6. Ibid.
7. Ibid.
8. Ibid., Nr.4, 15 February 1944, Ziff.86.

**DIENSTGRADABZEICHEN**
Badges of rank
The Waffen-SS inherited the badges of rank from its predecessors the Allgemeine-SS and SS-Verfügungstruppe, which were by tradition those of the SA. On mobilisation the armed SS had been given a specific role alongside the armed forces and it became essential, for practical and disciplinary reasons, that SS ranks should correspond to those in the armed forces, and easily recognised by armed forces personnel. In March 1938, just before the German entry into Austria, the SS-Verfügungstruppe were ordered to wear army pattern shoulder straps. This departure from traditional SS badges of rank was as unwelcome to Himmler as it was to the army, and a lot of thought was given in SS circles to an independent development of SS badges of rank. One written proposal,[1] suggested that 'since the SS has acquired such a reputation in this war, and its own identity, we can, and indeed must, detach ourselves from the armed forces in titles and badges of rank'.
The armed forces were dismayed by the increasing numbers of para-military personnel parading in the streets wearing uniforms and badges of rank which could be mistaken for those of the armed forces. After all, the German soldier was at a loss to know who he was supposed to salute, and, conversely, was not getting the salutes to which he was entitled. The OKW attempted to place

restrictions on the wearing of its uniforms and badges of rank, and the SS found the reasons most interesting 'on one hand it is said that the high loss of officers in action is because they are still too easily recognised, and on the other that the shoulder strap displays the combat badges by which the soldier recognises his officer in battle'. . . 'This can easily be refuted for no one will claim that the parachutists did not fight as well as the army, and yet they recognised their leaders and officers very well, by means of a small stripe on the sleeve.'

The proposal continued : 'Now I am of the opinion that the SS must take a big step forward here, and am convinced that in the war of the future the leader will only be recognised with great difficulty. I think it is right, therefore, that we in the SS should introduce the badges of rank that the parachutist wears on his jump smock*. If the German recruit recognises an Oberleutnant of parachutists and salutes him, then it will also be easy to recognise the Obersturmführer of the Waffen-SS wearing the same badges.'

'These badges would be worn on the uniform shirt, field blouse, greatcoat, and camouflage jacket. The question now arises as to whether or not the SS officer will continue to wear his badges of rank on the collar patch. One could answer this in the affirmative, because the camouflage jacket, which is part of the field uniform, conceals the collar patches. The field uniform is in itself very bad, and the retention of the collar patches would make it a little smarter when worn on its own behind the front. In any case, the national emblem on the left sleeve, and the SS runes collar patch for men, will remain. If one should not concede that officers continue to wear their badges of rank on the collar patch, they then would also wear the SS runes, or in the case of the SS-Totenkopf-Division, the death's head on both collar patches.'[2]
The OKW was still attempting to restrict the use of its basic uniform colours and badges of rank, but it was not until a special case arose, that Hitler in his capacity as Commander-in-Chief of the Armed Forces was compelled 'to express his opinion clearly on the wearing of military badges of rank and the uniforms of the armed forces'.[3] The following three relevant paragraphs are interesting.

*This or a similar proposal was taken up by the Waffen-SS, but the army was also thinking along similar lines, and in August 1942 introduced a special series of badges of rank for wear on uniforms without shoulder straps. These same badges were then officially adopted by the Waffen-SS in February 1943, although a semi-official series had been in use prior to that date.

(1) Military badges of rank are reserved solely and exclusively for bearers of military weapons (Militärische Waffenträger), i.e., the armed forces including the Waffen-SS.

(3) Military badges of rank may only be worn by those who have been through the various stages of military training within the branches of the armed forces or the Waffen-SS. These badges of rank establish a superiority which authorises the wearer to exercise his authority at all times, but especially in action. This authority must be based on military ability, leadership-wise, (e.g., a dentist is not a colonel, just as a colonel is not a dentist!)

(7) With regard to the SS the Führer has ordered that the basic colour of the SS uniform in peacetime will, once again, be black. The Waffen-SS, as state forces (Staatstruppe), will also wear black on garrison service. Field-grey is only to be worn by state forces on field service. Military badges of rank are only to be worn by these state forces, and not in the branches of the Allgemeine-SS.

The Führer concluded that he 'hopes that there will now be an end to the increase in the disorder regarding the wearing of military badges of rank for the duration of the war, and has ordered a radical clarification of this question after the war'.

**Notes:**

1. Undated draft report with pencilled amendments, possibly by Berger, on suggested development of the SS uniform, from the files of the Adjutantur of the SS-Hauptamt. On page 7 the strength of the Waffen-SS is given as 100,000 (amended 120,000). The official strength of the Waffen-SS on 4 May 1940 was 124,199.

2. Ibid. — This concession appears to have been granted, then almost immediately revoked. The original Verfügungstruppe and Totenkopf units continued to wear the runes or death's head on the right and badge of rank on the left collar patch. Elements of the newly formed divisions Totenkopf and Wiking were issued with (or purchased) collar patches with the runes or death's head on both sides. Despite the fact that numerous and categoric orders were issued in May 1940 forbidding this practice, it continued throughout 1942, possibly longer.

3. Adjutantur der Wehrmacht beim Führer, Oberst d.G.Schmundt an den Herrn Chef O.K.W. (abschriftlich an SS-Gruf. Wolff, desgl. RF-SS) Betr.: Militärische Rangabzeichen und Uniformen, Führer-Hauptquartier, den 9 November 1941.

# SS-VT/WAFFEN-SS BADGES OF RANK (DIENSTGRADABZEICHEN) 1939-1940. *

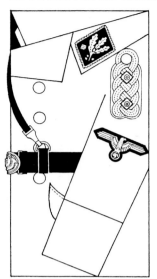

SS-Obergruppenführer
u. Gen. d. W.-SS

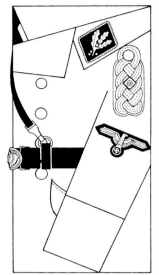

SS-Gruppenführer
u. Gen. Lt. d. W.-SS

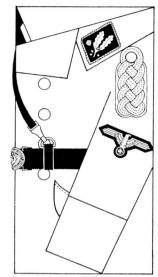

SS-Brigadeführer
u. Gen. Maj. d. W.-SS

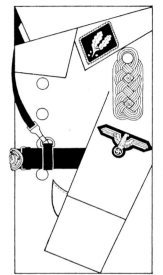

SS-Oberführer

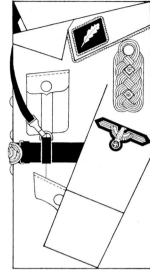

SS-Standartenführer

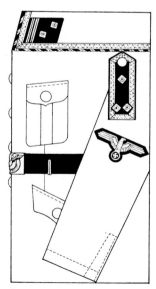

SS-Sturmscharführer

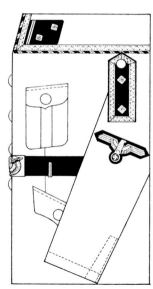

SS-Hauptscharführer

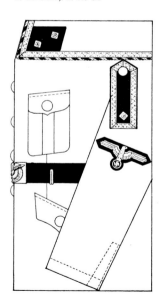

SS-Oberscharführer

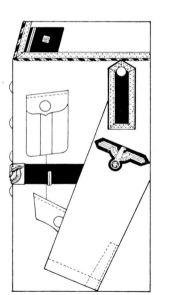

SS-Scharführer

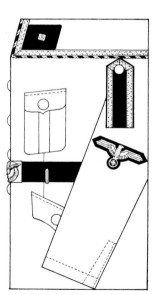

SS-Unterscharführer

*Despite orders to the contrary, collar patches were seldom piped in black and aluminium twisted cord, whereas the piping was still retained on the collar. Other ranks shoulder straps with pointed ends and officer's without the black underlay were still the most common in 1940.

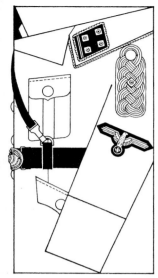

SS-Obersturmbannführer

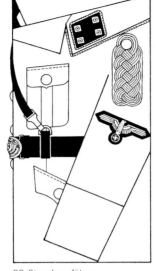

SS-Sturmbannführer

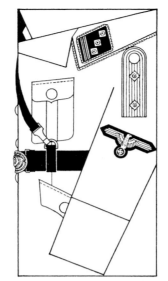

SS-Hauptsturmführer

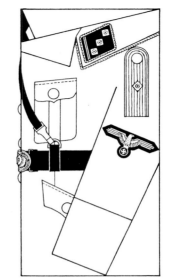

SS-Obersturmführer

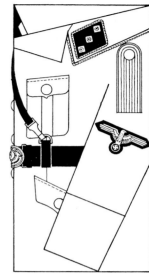

SS-Untersturmführer

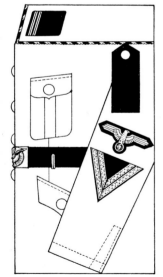

SS-Rottenführer

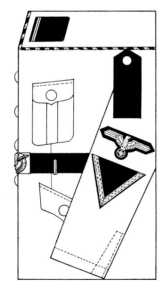

SS-Sturmmann

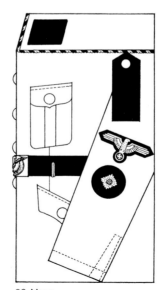

SS-Mann
SS-Oberschütze u.s.w.

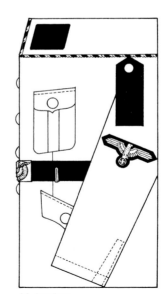

SS-Anwärter
SS-Schütze u.s.w.

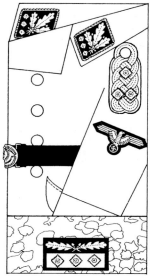

SS-Oberst-Gruppenführer
u. Gen. Obst. d. W.-SS

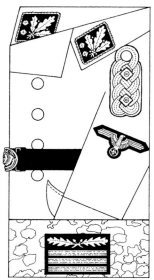

SS-Obergruppenführer
u. Gen. d. W.-SS

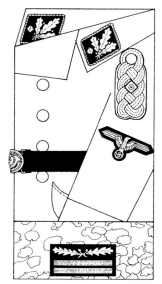

SS-Gruppenführer
u. Gen. Lt. d. W.-SS

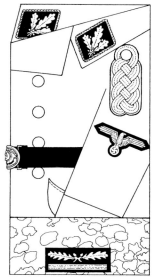

SS-Brigadeführer
u. Gen. Maj. d. W.-SS

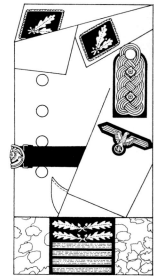

SS-Oberführer

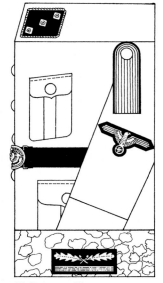

SS-Untersturmführer

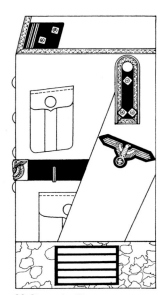

SS-Sturmscharführer

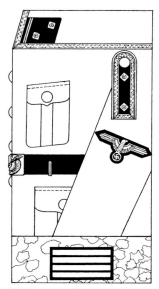

SS-Hauptscharführer

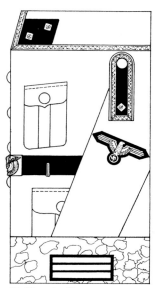

SS-Oberscharführer

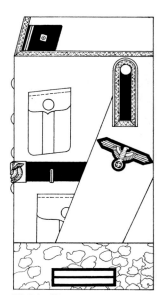

SS-Scharführer

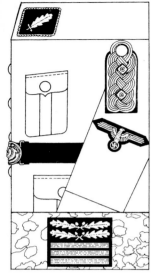

SS-Standartenführer

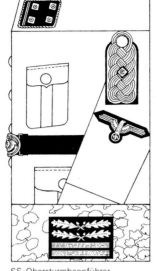

SS-Obersturmbannführer

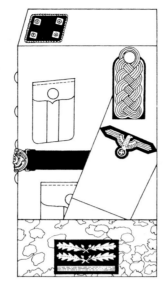

SS-Sturmbannführer

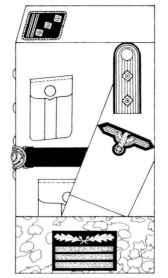

SS-Hauptsturmführer

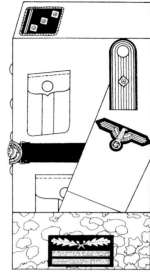

SS-Obersturmführer

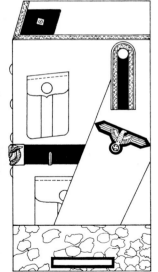

SS-Unterscharführer

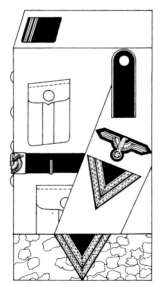

SS-Rottenführer

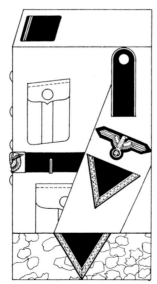

SS-Sturmmann

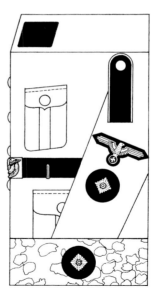

SS-Oberschütze u.s.w.

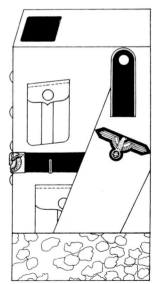

SS-Schütze u.s.w.

89

## DIENSTGRADABZEIBHEN FUR DEN FÜHRERNACHWUCHS DER WAFFEN-SS

Badges of rank for officer candidates of the Waffen-SS

At first, officer candidates (SS-Führeranwärter) wore their badges of rank and the insignia of their former units,[1] but by March 1935, however, officer cadets had been given special titles which corresponded to non-commissioned officer ranks in the SS.[2] Graduate officer cadets (SS-Standartenoberjunker) awaiting promotion to SS-Untersturmführer wore officer's uniform with the badges of rank (collar patches and shoulder straps) of an SS-Hauptscharführer.

It appears that officer cadets who had completed a war course at officers' school (Kriegslehrgang) with the rank of SS-Oscha. or SS-Hscha. were wearing officer's cords on their caps, together with N.C.O.'s insignia and lace. The SS-FHA. was obliged to point out that only those who had completed a full course (Voll-Lehrgang) at officers' school were to be promoted to SS-Stand.Ob.Ju., which entitled them to wear officer's cords and belt.[3] This distinction between those who intended to make their career in the Waffen-SS and those who had only joined for the duration of the war was soon abolished, and all graduates from officers' school were first made SS-Standartenoberjunker (d.Res.) before being promoted to SS-Untersturmführer (d.Res.) etc.

The privilege of wearing an officer's cap with N.C.O. badges of rank and lace was extended to Reserve Officer Candidates on promotion to SS-Hauptscharführer der Reserve in the medical or veterinary service. This compared to the armed forces ranks of Unterarzt and Unterveterinär.[4] When wearing service dress it was difficult to distinguish an officer cadet from an ordinary N.C.O., and so in February 1944 it was decided to introduce a new badge for all potential officers and officer cadets.[5]

## 268. Introduction of a badge for officer candidates in the Waffen-SS.

The Reichsführer-SS has ordered:

To identify active officer candidates, and reserve officer candidates (des Beurlaubtenstandes), the following badge is to be introduced forthwith:
Two field-grey artificial silk N.C.O.'s lace bars sewn together and worn across the base of the shoulder strap.

The badge is to be made from the stocks of the units concerned.

The following officer applicants (Führerbewerber) are entitled to wear the badge:

(a) Führerbewerber who have been ordered to a preparatory course, upon posting to that course.

(b) Führerbewerber who have completed the preparatory course and upon their posting to a War Cadets Course or War Reserve Officer Candidates Course, and until his promotion to SS-Stand. Ob.Ju.

(c) Führerbewerber who have completed the Reserve Officer Candidates course, upon their appointment to Reserve Officer Candidate (Reserve-Führer-Anwärter), and until their promotion to SS-Ustuf.d.Res.

Führerbewerber who are removed from the list of Führerbewerber or are discharged from the preparatory course or War Cadet or War Reserve Officer Candidates course, must remove the badge at once, even if they are proposed to enrol in a course again. The badge may be worn again, as and when they are posted to their respective course.

Concerning the entitlement to wear the above-mentioned badge, the Führerbewerber is to be issued with a pass, as per the following sample, which is to be signed by the commander of the school or unit concerned, or by his deputy, and bears the service seal.

### Sample

The. . . . . . . . . . . . . . . . . . . . . . . . as a Führerbewerber is authorised to wear the badge of an officer candidate of the Waffen-SS

Service seal                                                     Signature

SS-FHA/Amtsgr.B/AmtXX XI

An Estonian SS-Standartenoberjunker, wearing officer's cap (with non-regulation national emblem) and belt. The badges on his left breast pocket are Estonian.

Officer cadets (SS-Junker) at the funeral of SS-Brigaf. Fritz Witt, killed near Caen on 12 June 1944. Although technically cadets held N.C.O. rank they are not wearing gloves. They all wear the cuff-band of their former unit, to which they will return, and not that of the school.

**1940-1944**

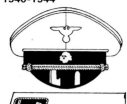
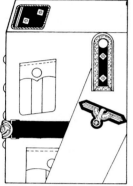
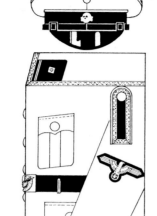

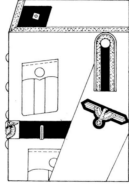

SS-Standartenoberjunker
(SS-Hscha.)

SS-Standartenjunker
(SS-Scha.)

SS-Junker (SS-Uscha.)

SS-Sturmmann (FB)

SS-Anwärter (FB)
SS-Schütze u.s.w. (FB)

**Feb. 1944-May 1945**

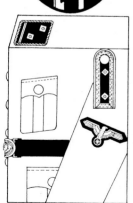
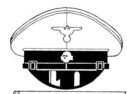
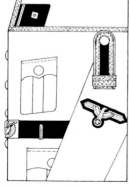

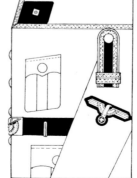
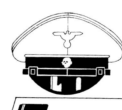
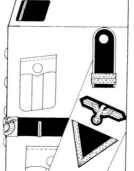
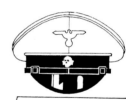
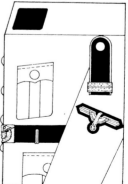

SS-Standartenoberjunker
(SS-Hscha.)

SS-Standartenjunker
(SS-Scha.)

SS-Junker (SS-Uscha.)

SS-Sturmmann (FB)

SS-Schütze u.s.w. (FB)

92

See note at foot of page 86

# WAFFEN-SS POTENTIAL OFFICERS AND OFFICER CADETS, BADGES OF RANK (DIENSTGRADABZEICHEN), RESERVE, 1940-1945.

**1940-1944**

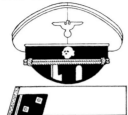
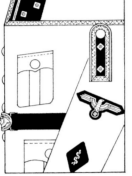
SS-Hauptscharführer
d. Res. (RFA)

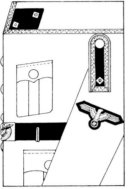
SS-Oberscharführer
d. Res. (RFA)

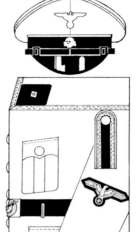
SS-Unterscharführer
d. Res. (RFA)

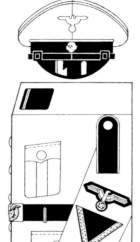
SS-Sturmmann (RFB)

SS-Anwärter (RFB)
SS-Schütze u.s.w. (RFB)

**Feb. 1944-May 1945**

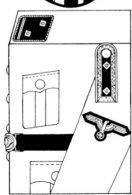
SS-Standartenoberjunker
**d. Res.**

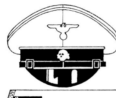
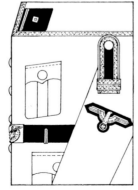
SS-Standartenjunker d. Res.

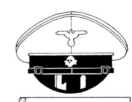
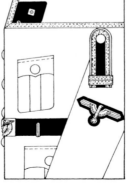
SS-Junker d. Res.

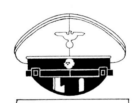
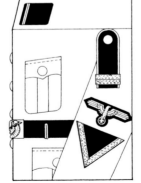
SS-Sturmmann (RFB)

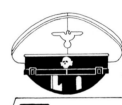
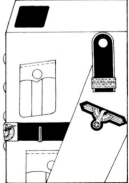
SS-Schütze u.s.w. (RFB)

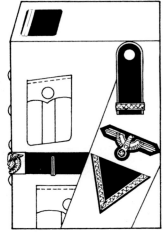

SS-Sturmmann and
SS-Unterfuhreranwarter
(12 yrs. service)

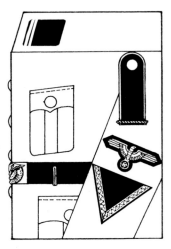

SS-Sturmmann and
SS-Unterfuhreranwarter
(less than 12 yrs. service)

## UNTERFÜHRER-ANWÄRTER-ABZEICHEN
Potential N.C.O.s badges

### 78. Potential N.C.O.s badges. [6]
It has been established that the badge for potential N.C.O.s who have signed on for twelve years, is being worn by other ranks not entitled to it. The potential N.C.O.'s badge is :

(a)  For potential N.C.O.s who hae signed on for twelve years ;
   a 0.9 cm wide, regulation aluminium lace bar across the bottom of the shoulder strap.

(b)  For potential N.C.O.s who have signed on for less than twelve years ;
   a 0.4 cm thick twisted cotton cord in Waffenfarbe across the bottom of the shoulder strap.

Only other ranks who have successfully completed a potential N.C.O.'s course (Unterführeranwärterlehrgang) are entitled to wear this badge, or if, because of their conduct in the ranks, they have been recommended for appointment to a potential N.C.O. by their company or battalion commander.

If a year after their attendance at the course a potential N.C.O. has not become a section commander (Gruppenführer), he must remove the badge.

Kdo.d.W.-SS IIb

### Kragenspiegel
Collar patches

In February 1938 the introduction of army badges of rank rendered the SS collar patches, which denoted both the rank and formation of the wearer, superfluous. In the Waffen-SS, badges of rank, branch of service, and formation insignia (Cyphers, numerals, and letters) could all appear on the shoulder strap. In addition, the formation name or designation already appeared on the cuff-band.

An order of 10 May 1940 concerning the field-grey uniform of the Waffen-SS (issued on day Germany invaded western Europe) rendered obsolete, for security reasons, all the pre-war SS-VT and SS-TV collar patches with the SS runes or death's head with numerals and letters. From that date on, the SS

### Notes:
1.  SS-Befehls-Blatt., Nr.10, 15 October 1934, Nr.5.
2.  Ibid., Nr.3, 25 March 1935, Nr.16.
3.  V.Bl.d.W.-SS., Nr.12, 1 November 1940, Ziff.297.
4.  Ibid., Nr.23, 15 December 1941, Ziff.487.
5.  Ibid., Nr.4, 15 February 1944, Ziff.86.
6.  Ibid., Nr.24, 15 December 1941, Ziff.78.

runes and the death's head became the standard collar patches of the Waffen-SS.[1] The change-over from the old pattern to the new could not take place over night, and as an interim measure units serving in the front-line with old collar patches removed them. Since one collar patch could hardly be worn on its own, they removed both.[2] To complicate matters even further, other units, mainly those in the Totenkopf Division, were still wearing the double death's head.

Allgemeine-SS badges of rank, as worn in the Waffen-SS, remained unchanged until April 1942, when the Führer approved the introduction of a new rank — SS-Oberst-Gruppenführer — and corresponding badges of rank. This, however, entailed the alteration of the design of the existing collar patches for the ranks SS-Staf. — SS-Ogruf. There were no further changes to the design of SS collar patches for the rest of the war.

## Manufacture

SS collar patches were made in the shape of a parallelogram (60 x 40 mm) consisting of a piece of buckram (or metal for the removable ones), covered in black badge cloth or felt for all ranks up to and including SS-Obersturmbannführer and black velvet for all ranks from SS-Standartenführer to SS-Oberst-Gruppenführer. The collar patch was usually sewn to the collar of the tunic, field blouse, or greatcoat, unless it was the removable pattern with metal base and a screw fitting at each corner, in which case it was screwed to the collar.

Before the war and until August 1940 the collar patch for other ranks was edged in 1½ mm black and aluminium twisted cord.[4] Officers' collar patches were edged in 1½ mm aluminium twisted cord, although during the war this was often omitted from the collar patches on the field uniform. All ranks from SS-Unterscharführer up to and including SS-Obersturmbannführer were identified by 12 mm aluminium stars (maximum 4); intermediary ranks had in addition 6 mm wide aluminium lace with a black stripe (maximum 2). Oak leaves for the ranks SS-Standartenführer up to and including SS-Oberst-Gruppenführer were hand-embroidered in aluminium wire, as were the 1 cm sq. stars. Metal stars were never worn on collar patches by general officers.

## Notes:

1. V.Bl.d.W.-SS., Nr.23, 15 December 41, Ziff.482.
2. See photographs in Waffen-SS im Westen.
3. Der Reichsführer-SS, Tgb.N.RF/V.Betr. Dienstgradabzeichen der SS und Polizei. Führer-Hauptquartier, 7 April 1942.
4. V.Bl.d.W.-SS., Nr.18, 15 August 1940, Ziff. 155.

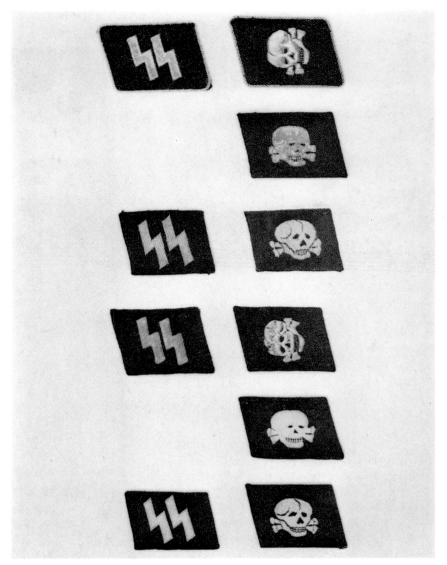

Development of the SS runes and death's head collar patches. L-R: 1st pattern hand embroidered SS runes and death's head for officers. This pattern was worn on both collar patches. 2nd pattern hand embroidered death's head for officers; also worn in pairs. Final pattern for officers, woven in aluminium thread.
1st pattern machine embroidered SS runes and death's head for other ranks. The death's head was worn on both collar patches. 1940 pattern machine embroidered death's head which was also worn in pairs. Final machine woven pattern for other ranks.

Top L-R: Standard RZM version of the post-1942 hand-embroidered collar patch for SS-Obergruppenführer and SS-Oberführer. Collar patch for SS-Obersturmführer with regulation stars and intermediary rank lace.
Bottom L-R: Standard RZM version of the pre-1942 hand embroidered collar patch for SS-Brigadeführer and SS-Standartenführer. Collar patch for SS-Untersturmführer with non-regulation stars.

## Schulterstücke (Führer)
### Shoulder straps (commissioned ranks)

In July 1935 officers of the SS-Verfügungstruppe were ordered to wear Allgemeine-SS shoulder cords on both shoulders (see Vol. 3, pp. 48–50) of their earth-grey, and later field-grey tunics, blouses and greatcoats. They were worn until March 1938, when the army pattern was introduced. At first, SS officers purchased army officer's shoulder straps with either matt or bright aluminium braid on a white underlay, with gilt metal stars.

The December 1939 order stated that the army pattern shoulder straps were to be in matt aluminium braid (bright aluminium was forbidden), and that the underlay was to be in the basic colour of the SS (black) for all officers in all

units. In addition, army Waffenfarbe piping was to be worn between the braid and the black underlay. General officers were to have general's pattern braiding (two gilt and one aluminium) on a light silver grey underlay only. Company and field officers were to have 20 mm bronzed and general officers 26 mm stars in silvered metal.[1]

Introduction of army shoulder straps was the most radical departure from the predominantly political tradition of the SS uniform.* No sooner had they been introduced than the question immediately arose as to which SS officers (particularly those in the SS-Hauptamt) were to consider themselves members of the Waffen-SS, and thus eligible to wear them. On 14 May 1939, SS-Oberf. Frank, chief of the Verwaltungsamt-SS, was informed that 'the Reichsführer-SS does not want, apart from the Inspector of the SS-Verfügungstruppe, SS-Brigaf. Hausser, other SS general officers in the SS-VT and SS-TV, to wear army shoulder straps. The wearing of army shoulder straps by officers up to the rank of SS-Staf. in the SS-VT and SS-TV is permitted by the Reichsführer-SS.[2]

*After the war Himmler was in favour of reintroducing the pre-war black service uniform complete with its single shoulder cord, but realised that this might not be very popular with an officer of the Waffen-SS, who was only eligible to receive the 'comradely salute' from members of the armed forces when wearing army badges of rank. To allow Waffen-SS personnel to wear army shoulder straps on the black uniform would have meant dividing the Waffen-SS from the Allgemeine-SS, which was, after all, the foundation of the SS order. This solution also created other problems. A retired Waffen-SS officer would automatically become a member of the Allgemeine-SS and would only be entitled to wear Allgemeine-SS uniform and badges of rank. The proposed solution to this problem was the introduction of standard shoulder straps with the national emblem embroidered in aluminium wire for officers and white silk for men. These shoulder straps would not denote the wearer's rank, but would identify him as an ex-member of the Waffen-SS. His rank would continue to appear on the collar patch.[5]

Three of these shoulder straps have survived the war, and until now defied identification. There are two distinct types. The first is $4\frac{1}{2}$ cm wide with gilt embroidery and a gilt metal button bearing the SS runes. The second is slightly narrower ($3\frac{1}{2}$ cm) with silver embroidery and a white metal death's head button. The wider gilt pattern may have been intended for general officers, while the death's head button may have denoted ex-members of the SS-Totenkopfverbände.

On 13 December 1939 Himmler sent the following directive to all his Main Office Chiefs:[3]

'I refer to my order concerning the introduction of Reserve Waffen-SS officers, and request that Main Office Chiefs ensure, with all powers at their disposal, that no SS leader under their command wears Waffen-SS shoulder straps on his service dress unless entitled to do so. The following are so entitled:

(1)  Waffen-SS officers

(2)  Reserve Waffen-SS officers

(3)  Security Police and SD leaders on active duty; regarding those people who are to be included in this category, please inquire to the Chief of the SD-Hauptamt

(4)  Certain of your Main Office Chiefs, as proposed by the SS-Personal-hauptamt, and with my personal approval.

On 10 May 1940 Himmler amended his December 1939 order as follows. Officers' shoulder straps were to remain the same with black underlay and army Waffenfarbe piping, but the metal insignia was to be in bronzed metal for all company and field officers, and silvered metal for general officers with the rank of SS-Brigaf. and above. The old gilt insignia could be worn until 31 December 1940 at the latest.[4] In fact it was worn until the end of the war.

**Notes:**

1.  See Appendix I.

2.  Der Chef des SS-Hauptamtes, SS-Gruf. Heissmeyer an SS-Oberf. Frank, Chef des Verwaltungsamt-SS, und SS-Führungsamt. Inspekteur der SS-Verfügungstruppe und Führer der SS-Totenkopfverbände, Berlin, den 14 May 1939.

3.  Der Reichsführer-SS, Über das SS-Hauptamt zur Verteilung an alle Hauptämter, Berlin, den 13 December 1939.

4.  See Appendix II.

5.  Undated draft report with pencilled amendments, possibly by Berger, on suggested development of the SS uniform, from the files of the Adjutantur des SS-Hauptamtes.

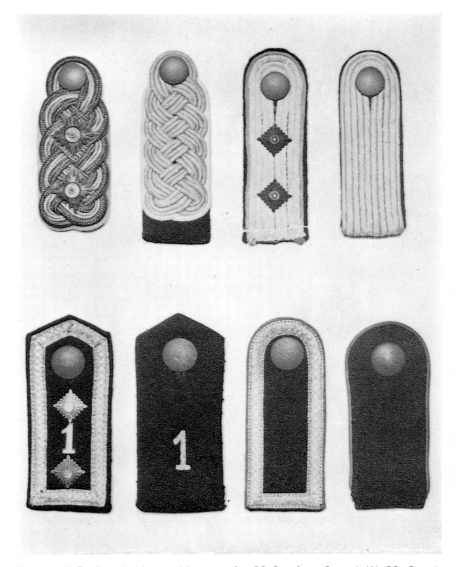

Top row, L-R: Detachable shoulder strap for SS-Ogruf. u. Gen. d. W.-SS. Sew-in pattern for SS-Sturmbannführer and SS-Hauptsturmführer and detachable pattern for SS-Untersturmführer.
Bottom row, L-R: Pre-1939 SS-VT and Waffen-SS pattern shoulder strap for SS-Hauptscharführer and other ranks (Mannschaftsdienstgrade). Post 1939 Waffen-SS pattern for SS-Scharführer and other ranks.

Prototype SS shoulder boards for wear on black uniform to distinguish ex-members of the Waffen-SS.

### Schulterklappen

Shoulder straps (other ranks)

In July 1935 all members of the SS-VT were ordered to replace their Allgemeine-SS shoulder cord by army pattern shoulder straps (measuring $11\frac{1}{2} \times 4\frac{1}{2}$ cm) on both shoulders of the earth-grey field tunic.[1] At first these were made of earth-grey, and later black cloth with rounded ends, edged in 2 mm black and white or 1.5 mm black and aluminium twisted cord: they did not however identify the wearer's rank.

In March 1938 N.C.O.s began to wear aluminium lace and 20 mm white metal stars on their shoulder straps, which by this date existed in two distinct patterns. The first was made of black cloth with rounded ends and black and aluminium twisted cord piping. The second was made of a coarser quality black cloth with pointed ends and no piping. This pattern was intended for wear with the field blouse, and had a tongue which passed through a loop on the blouse or greatcoat and fastened with a button.

In December 1939 new black cloth shoulder straps with rounded ends and piping in army Waffenfarben were introduced.[2] During the ensuing change-over a limited number of shoulder straps with pointed ends and piping were manufactured and issued.[3] In May 1940 it was announced that as soon as field units had been issued with the new shoulder straps, replacement units were to receive them.[4] Also in 1940 lace began to be manufactured in mouse grey or field-grey artificial silk.

### Notes:

1. Der Chef des SS-Hauptamtes an SS-Oberabschnitte und SS-Verfügungstruppen, Berlin, 27 July 1935, Betr.: Erdgraue Röcke.
2. See Appendix I.
3. See Waffen-SS im Westen, one from last page, with illustration.
4. V.Bl.Insp.(E)., Nr.3, 1 May 1940.

### Dienstgradabzeichen für Mannschaftendienstgrade

Badges of rank for other ranks

Army badges of rank for the lowest SS ranks are believed to have been introduced in March 1938, at the same time as the army pattern shoulder straps.[1] They were worn on the upper left sleeve $1\frac{1}{2}$ cm under the national emblem on all but camouflage uniforms.[2] In February 1943 the wearing of these badges on camouflage uniform was officially permitted.[3]

### Manufacture

SS-Mann/SS-Oberschütze u.s.w. Machine-embroidered 2 cm-sq. star in silver grey artificial silk thread on a circular black cloth ground.
SS-Sturmmann. One 9 mm wide lace chevron on a triangular black cloth.
SS-Rottenführer. Two 9 mm wide lace chevrons on a triangular black cloth.

The 9 mm lace was at first woven in aluminium wire, but from 1940 onwards it was also manufactured in either mouse grey or field-grey artificial silk thread for wear on the field uniform, or sand coloured thread for tropical uniform. The two chevrons for SS-Rottenführer were also woven in one piece.

**Notes:**
1. The exact date of introduction has denied confirmation to date. It was certainly earlier than 1940 (see Taylor/Bender, Vol. 1, p. 110) since a photo of the Leibstandarte in the market place at Eger in October 1938 shows an SS-Sturmmann wearing the single chevron. It seems logical that once it had been agreed to adopt army badges of rank the SS would have adopted them all, and not in stages as hitherto generally accepted. FM-Zeitschrift., Folge 11, Berlin 1 November 1938.
2. This conflicted with the wearing of the national shield (Landesschild) and so in April 1944, the regulation was amended, so that the shield should be worn under the national emblem, and the rank badge under the shield. V.Bl.d.W.-SS., Nr.8, 15 April 1944, Ziff.164.
3. Ibid., Nr.4, 15 February 1944, Ziff.63.

### Dienstgradabzeichen an Bekleidungsstücken ohne Schulterstücke bzw. Schulterklappen.

Badges of rank on clothing without shoulder straps

No sooner had camouflage uniform been generally adopted than difficulty in identifying rank was soon encountered in the field. As early as May 1940 the use of strips of lace or cloth on the sleeve, already in use in the air-force was advocated.[1] At the beginning of the Russian campaign officers of the SS-Aufkl.Abt. (and possibly other units) identified their rank group by strips of white tape or aluminium lace on the upper sleeves of their camouflage smock.[2] This system is believed to have been that originally introduced in 1936 for motorised units of the SS-VT for wear on overalls and greatcoats.[3] It consisted of strips of aluminium braid for overalls, and white rubber for the rubberised motor-cyclists coat. Each stripe was 1 cm wide by 8 cm long and the distance between each stripe was 0.3 cm. In September 1937 the original order was amended, so that the stripes went right round the arm.[4]

| SS-Unterführer | N.C.O.s | One stripe |
| SS-Führer | Company officers | Two stripes |
| SS-Stabsführer | Field officers | Three stripes |

The German army was faced with a similar problem, and designed and introduced a completely new system of badges of rank in August 1942. In February 1943 these same badges (with minor differences) were introduced in the Waffen-SS.[5]

Top row, L-R: Sleeve star for SS-Oberschütze etc., and chevrons in mouse-grey artificial silk, regulation pattern, lace for SS-Rottenführer.
Badges of rank for uniforms without shoulder straps, L-R: SS-Gruf. with oak leaves machine embroidered in yellow artificial silk thread, and yellow cellophane lace bars. SS-Untersturmführer in green artificial silk thread and green cellophane bars. Bottom row: Printed pattern in black on bright green artificial silk ground for SS-Sturmbannführer and SS-Oberscharführer.

Officers of the SS-Aufkl.Abt. interrogate a captured Soviet officer during the opening stages of the invasion of Russia. The SS-Hauptsturmführer on the right is identified by two bars on both sleeves of his camouflage smock.

**63. Badges of rank for clothing without shoulder straps.**

1. To identify the rank of officers and N.C.O.s of the Waffen-SS on the:
   Snow and fur anorak
   Sheepskin
   Winter combination for Panzer troops
   Drill uniform, black and reed green
   Camouflage jacket
   Camouflaged combination for Panzer troops
   Drill jacket
   Tropical shirt
   Training costume (sports), and working dress
   Special machine-embroidered badges on an oblong black ground (as illustrated in Appendix II) are introduced, and are for:
   (a) Generals of the Waffen-SS, in golden yellow
   (b) Officers, including SS-Oberf., in bright green
   (c) N.C.O.s, in bright green.
2. Position of the badges: Upper left sleeve — top of the badge 10 cm from the shoulder seam. On clothing without shoulder seams the badge is to be worn at the same height as on clothing with the seams.
3. The wearing of other badges of rank on those items of clothing listed under para. 1 is not permitted.
4. Other ranks wear the same badges of rank on those items of clothing listed under para. 1 as on the field-grey and drill uniforms.
5. Units and offices are to indent for their requirements as follows:
   (a) Officers in a collective order from the SS-Clothing Counter, Berlin-Wilmersdorf, Kaiserallee 42;
   (b) Other ranks via the normal clothing supply channels.

SS-FHA./Amt II/Ia

Long after the introduction of these badges of rank shoulder straps and other insignia continued to be worn on camouflage clothing.

**381. Badges of rank on camouflage clothing.** [6]

Shoulder straps are not to be worn on uniforms made from camouflage drill material. Only those badges of rank published in V.B.d.W.-SS., Nr.4, 15 February 1943, Ziff.63 are to be worn.

SS-FHA./Ia

**Manufacture**

The 9 cm-long oak leaves were machine-embroidered in either golden yellow or bright green artificial silk thread on a rectangular black badge cloth ground. [7] The 9 cm-long bars were made of a 1 cm wide golden yellow or bright green cellophane lace. The badge for SS-Oberst-Gruppenführer was unique in that it had a single 2 cm-wide golden yellow lace bar, on which was machine-embroidered in silver grey silk, three 20 mm stars. A cheaper version for all ranks up to and including SS-Oberführer were screen printed in black on bright green artificial silk. Although hitherto this pattern was presumed to have been made since the war, those in the author's collection came from a huge stock found in Paris, and their originality can be confirmed by comparison with that shown in the illustration opposite.

### Notes:

1. Undated draft report with pencilled amendments on suggested improvements to SS uniform from the files of the Adjutantur des SS-Hauptamtes., May 1940.
2. See illustration on p. 100, and Die Deutsche Wehrmacht, Heft 12, with an illustration which in fact shows an SS officer (with two white bars, on his camouflage combination) and not an SS-Oberscharführer as stated.
3. SS-Befehls-Blatt., Nr.4, 25 June 1936, Nr.2.
4. Ibid., Nr.9, 25 August 1937, Nr.2.
5. V.Bl.d.W.-SS., Nr.4, 15 February 1943, Ziff.63.
6. Ibid., Nr.14, 15 July 1944, Ziff.381.
7. See illustration on p. 102 which shows the special pattern for working overalls.

### WAFFENFARBEN
Branch of service colours

Until the introduction of army shoulder straps, the question of Waffenfarbe had not arisen in the SS-Verfügungstruppe. All piping on SS uniform (peaked cap and long trousers) was white, irrespective of the wearer's branch of service. With the adoption of army shoulder straps with underlay in Waffenfarbe, officers began to equip themselves with peaked caps and long trousers with coloured piping. The attached amendments to the first SS order concerning the field-grey uniform of the Waffen-SS, dated 12 December 1939, clearly state, however, that the piping on peaked caps and trousers was to remain white.[1] The next order dated 10 May 1940, states that the trousers are to be uniformly piped in a grey colour and the peaked cap in Waffenfarbe. It concluded by ordering that the correct Waffenfarbe be adopted immediately, and that items not conforming to this order may only be worn until 31 December 1940.[2]

On 5 November 1940 Himmler changed his mind once again amending his May 1940 order as follows:

SS-Hauptsturmführer Joseph Krämer commandant of Bergen-Belsen concentration camp after his capture by British troops. He wears an issue shirt with loop for shoulder straps and the printed pattern of badge of rank for wear on clothing without shoulder straps.

An SS-Hauptscharführer (left) and an SS-Obersturmführer of the Instand-setzungsstaffel des II. SS-Panzerkorps near Charkov, Spring 1943. They both wear the special version of badges of rank for working overalls.

1. The piping on the SS peaked cap for officers, N.C.O.s and men is white. Officers with the rank of SS-Oberführer and above are to have silver (aluminium) piping. Waffenfarbe is to appear only on the shoulder straps and field cap.
2. The aluminium piping on the officer's field cap is in future to be worn only SS-Oberführer and above. All other officers are to wear white piping.*
3. On the long grey trousers the piping is to be white.*
4. Items rendered obsolete by this order may be worn until 31 December 1940.[3]

Paragraph 2 appears to have been ignored, and there is no evidence or surviving examples of officers' field caps piped in white.

As the end of 1940 drew to a close, SS officers, who by this time must have been in some doubt as to what exactly they were supposed to wear, were reminded that:

### 439. Application of Waffenfarbe [4]

The RF-SS has ordered, that all officers of the Waffen-SS, must in accordance with my order of the 10.5.1940, have the shoulder straps with the correct piping of their unit, by the 1 January 1941. (See in this respect the order of the RF-SS Hauptamt für Haushalt und Bauten — 1/3 1501 — of the 19.6.40).

The continued wearing of non-regulation shoulder straps, or those with the incorrect Waffenfarbe beyond the 31.12.1940 is hereby forbidden.

This equally applies to the field equipment for N.C.O.s and men.

With regards to the wearing of white piping on the peaked cap and long trousers, see the order of the RF-SS of the 5 Nov. 1940, according to which the wearing of those of a different manufacture also terminates on the 31.12.1940.

Kdo.der W.-SS/IVa

*Although permission to wear piping in Waffenfarbe on the peaked cap (and long trousers) had only been officially permitted for a matter of seven months, a large number of officers and men continued to wear it until the end of the war.

### Notes:

1. See Appendix I.
2. See Appendix II.
3. Der RF-SS u. ChdDtPol. SS-Befehl (Abschrift) Betr.: Feldgraue Uniform der Waffen-SS, Sipo. und des SD.Bezug.: Mein Befehl vom 10 May 1940, Berlin, den 5 November 1940.
4. V.Bl.d.W.-SS., Nr.15, 15 December 1940, Ziff.439.

| | November 1939[1] | May 1940[2] | June 1942[3] | Final[3a] |
|---|---|---|---|---|
| 1. White<br>Weiss | Infantry<br>Divisions-Stab<br>SS-Stand. Deutschland<br>SS-Stand. Germania<br>SS-Stand. Der Führer<br>Fla.MG.Abt.<br>1.-3. SS-T-Stand.<br>Leibstand-SS Adolf Hitler<br>Inspektion-SS-VT.<br>E-Einheiten der SS-VT u.SS-TV<br>Gruppenkommando der SS-TV.<br>Verstärkt SS-T-Stand.<br>SS-Rekruten-Stand.<br>Stamm der SS-Junkerschulen | Infantry<br>Divisionsstäbe<br>Leibst.SS-Adolf Hitler<br>SS-Deutschland<br>SS-Germania<br>SS-Der Führer<br>SS-Nordland<br>Fla.MG.Abt.<br>1.-3. SS-T-Standarte<br>Inspektion SS-VT(E)<br>Generalinspektion SS-T. Sta.<br>SS-Totenkopfstandarten<br>SS-Rekrutenstandarten<br>E-Einheiten der SS-VT u SS-T. Sta.<br>Stamm der SS-Junkerschulen u. der<br>Unterf.-Schule der SS-T.Sta. | Infantry<br>Divisionsstäbe<br>Infanterie<br>E-Einheiten | Infantry<br>Generalkommandos der Panzer-<br>Korps u.Divisionsstäbe<br>(Unterführer und Mann-<br>Schaften).[4]<br>Infanterie (Grenadier u.Pz. Gren.)<br>Stamm der Junkerschulen<br>Panzer-Grenadier-Schulen<br>Musikschule Braunschweig<br>E-Einheiten |
| 2. Bright red<br>Hochrot | Artillery<br>SS-Artillerie-Standarten der<br>SS-VT und SS-TV.<br>E-Einheiten | Artillery<br>SS-Artillerie-Standarten der<br>SS-VT und SS-TV.<br>E-Einheiten | Artillery<br>Artillerie<br>Flakeinheiten<br>E-Einheiten | Artillery<br>Artillerei<br>Flakeinheiten<br>Werfereinheiten<br>Artillerie-Schulen[5]<br>E-Einheiten |
| 3. Black<br>Schwarz | Engineers<br>Pioniersturmbanne der<br>SS-VT und SS-TV.<br>E-Einheiten | Engineers<br>Pionier-Sturmbanne der<br>SS-VT und SS-TV.<br>E-Einheiten | Engineers<br>Pioniereinheiten<br>E-Einheiten | Engineers<br>Pioniereinheiten[6]<br>Baueinheiten<br>Pionier-Schulen<br>E-Einheiten |
| 4. Lemon Yellow<br>Zitronengelb | Signals<br>Nachrichten-Abeitlungen<br>der SS-VT und SS-TV.<br>E-Einheiten | Signals<br>Nachrichten-Abteilungen der<br>SS-VT und SS-TV.<br>E-Einheiten | Signals<br>Nachrichteneinheiten<br>Kriegsberichter<br>E-Einheiten | Signals<br>Nachrichteneinheiten<br>Propaganda-Truppen<br>(Kriegsberichter)<br>Nachrichten-Schulen<br>E-Einheiten |
| 5. Pink<br>Rosa | Panzer<br>Panzer Abw.-Abt. der<br>SS-VT und SS-TV.<br>E-Einheiten | Panzer<br>Panzer-Abwehr-Abt.der<br>SS-VT und SS-TV.<br>E-Einheiten | Panzer<br>Panzer u.Panzerjäger-<br>Einheiten<br>E-Einheiten | Panzer<br>Panzer u.Panzerjäger-<br>Einheiten<br>Panzer-Schulen<br>E-Einheiten |

| No. | Colour | Column 1 | Column 2 | Column 3 | Column 4 |
|---|---|---|---|---|---|
| 6. | Copper brown<br>Kupferbraun | Reconnaissance<br>Aufklärungs-Abt. der<br>　SS-VT und SS-TV.<br>E-Einheiten | Reconnaissance<br>Aufklärungs.-Abt. der<br>　SS-VT und SS-TV.<br>E-Einheiten | | |
| 7. | Golden Yellow<br>Goldgelb | Cavalry<br>Reiterstandarten der<br>　SS-TV. | Cavalry<br>Reiterstandarten der<br>　SS-TV. | Cavalry<br>Reitereinheiten<br>Aufklärungseinheiten<br>E-Einheiten | Cavalry<br>Reitereinheiten<br>Aufklärungsabteilungen (mot.)<br>Kavallerie-Schulen<br>Reit-und Fahrschulen<br>E-Einheiten |
| 8. | Light blue<br>Hellblau | Transport and Supply<br>Verpflegsamt<br>Bäckerei<br>Schlächterei<br>Nachschub-Dienste<br>Werkstatt-Komp. | Transport and Supply<br>Verpflegsämter<br>Bäckereikolonnen<br>Schlächtereizüge<br>Nachschubdienste<br>Werkstatt-Komp. | Transport and Supply<br>Versorgungstruppen<br>　(Nachsch.-, Verw.-, u.<br>　Techn.Dienste) | Transport and Supply<br>Versorgungstruppen<br>　(Nachsch.-, Verw.-,u.<br>　Techn.Dienste)<br>SS-Feldpost[7] |
| 9. | Dark blue<br>Kornblumenblau | Medical<br>Sanitäts-Abteilung<br>Sanitäts-Einheiten<br>E-Einheiten | Medical<br>Sanitäts-Abteilung<br>Sanitäts-Einheiten<br>E-Einheiten<br>Ärzte u.San.Pers.d.Truppe.<br>Ärzte u.San.Pers.d.Lazarette | Medical<br>Sanitätsdienste<br>E-Einheiten | Medical<br>Sanitätsdienste<br>Sanitäts-Schulen<br>E-Einheiten |
| 10. | Orange<br>Orangerot | Recruiting<br>Ergänzungsstellen | Special Services<br>Angehörige der Sonderdienste<br>　(Verw.-,Gerichts.-Techn.-, u.<br>　Ergänzungsdienst u.d.Ang.d.<br>　Standortkommandanturen) [8] | Special Services<br>Technische Führer<br>　(Kraftfahr, Waffen<br>　u.Nachrichten)<br>Feldgendarmerie<br>Ergänzungsdienste<br>Fürsorgeführer | Special Services<br>Technische Führer<br>　(Kraftfahr, Waffen<br>　u.Machrichten)<br>Feldgendarmerie<br>Ergänzungsdienste<br>Fürsorgeführer |
| 11. | Light brown<br>Hellbraun | | Concentration Camps<br>Inspekteur der KL.<br>Kommandanturstäbe der KL.<br>KL-Verstärkung<br>KL-Totenkopfsturmbanne | Concentration Camps<br>Inspekteur der KL.<br>Kommandanturstäbe der KL<br>KL-Totenkopfwachsturmbanne | Concentration Camps<br>Inspekteur der KL<br>Kommandanturstäbe der KL<br>KL-Totenkopfwachsturmbanne |

| | | | |
|---|---|---|---|
| 12. Light grey<br>Hellgrau | Main Offices<br>Auf Planstellen des Reiches<br>eingestufte SS-Ang.bei den<br>SS-Hauptämstern bis einschl.<br>SS-Oberführer | Staff of the RF-SS<br>Persönlicher Stab<br>RF-SS | |
| | General Officers<br>Führer der Waffen-SS im<br>Generalsrang ab SS-Brigaf. | General Officers<br>Führer im Generalsrang<br>ab SS-Brigaf. | General Officers<br>Führer im Generalsrang<br>ab SS-Brigaf. |
| 13. Red and grey<br>Rotgrau | | Specialists<br>Fachführer | Specialists<br>Fachführer [9] |
| 14. Light salmon pink<br>Hell-Lachsrosa | | Military Geologists<br>Wehrgeologeneinheiten | Military Geologists<br>Wehrgeologeneinheiten |
| 15. Crimson<br>Karmesinrot | | Veterinary<br>Veterinärdienste | Veterinary<br>Veterinärdienste |
| 16. Claret<br>Bordeauxrot | | Legal Service<br>Gerichtsdienste | Legal Service<br>Gerichtsdienste |
| 17. Sky blue<br>Lichtblau | | Administration<br>Führer, U/Führer u.<br>Mannschaften der<br>Verwaltung | Administration<br>Führer, U/Führer u.<br>Mannschaften der<br>Verwaltung |
| 18. Dark grey<br>Dunkelgrau | | | Personal Staff RF-SS [10]<br>Persönliche Stab des RF-SS. |
| 19. Grass green<br>Wiesengrün | | | Mountain Troops [11]<br>Gebirgstruppen<br>Gebirgsjäger-Schulen<br>E-Einheiten |
| 20. Light pink<br>Hellrosa | | | Transport Troops [12]<br>Kraftfahrtruppen<br>Kraftfahr-Schulen<br>Kraftfahrtechnische<br>Lehranstalt [13]<br>E-Einheiten |

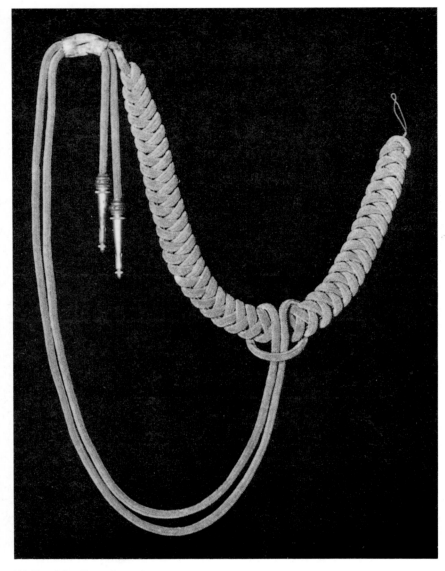

Waffen-SS adjutant's cords.

## Explanatory guide to the Waffenfarben listing

The listing is compiled chronologically by the date of introduction of each colour. The original listings have not been altered or corrected in any way despite known omissions. The final listing has been compiled from a number of different sources including Dich ruft die SS, p. 92, and the 1943 edition of Der Soldatenfreund (Ausgabe D:Waffen-SS), Tafel 17.

**Notes:**

1. Appendix 1 to the amendments to the RF-SS-Befehl vom 12 December 1939, HHB 1/3 009, Betr.: Feldgraue Uniform der Waffen-SS.

2. Appendix 1 to the RF-SS-Befehl (Abschrift) vom 10 May 1940, Betr.: Feldgraue Uniform der Waffen-SS, Sicherheitspolizei und des SD.

3. SS-Führungshauptamt Abt.Ia.Betr.: Waffenfarben der Waffen-SS (Abschrift), Berlin-Wilmersdorf, 30 May 1942, and supplement dated 19 June 1942.

4. Officers retained the Waffenfarbe of their former unit. V.Bl.d.W.-SS., Nr.17, 1 September 1943, Ziff.322.

5. Ibid., Nr.17, 1 September 1943, Ziff.307.

6. Ibid., Nr.13, 1 July 1944, Ziff.368.

7. Ibid., Nr.3, 1 February 1943, Ziff.37. Previously lemon yellow was worn.

8. Until the introduction of orange, staff retained the Waffenfarbe of their former unit. Der Chef des SS-Hauptamtes SS-Ogruf. Heissmeyer, Betr.: Abzeichen für die Angehörigen der SS-Standort-Kommandantur Prag, Berlin, den 7 March 1940.

9. Prior to the introduction of red and grey twisted cord piping for Fachführer in June 1942, officers and N.C.O.s in special service (Führer und Unterführer im Sonderdienst) wore dark green Waffenfarbe. RF-SS-Führungshauptamt, IIb/(1) Az.64: B 16 h Nr.221/11, 1941 vom 6 November 1941.

10. SS-Führungshauptamt Kdo.W-SS, Abt. Ia, gez. Jüttner, SS-Gruf.u. Gen.Lt.d.W.-SS. Betr.: Waffenfarben der Waffen-SS, Bezug.: SS-FHA, Abt. Ia, vom 30 May 1942. Berlin-Wilmersdorf, den 3 July 1942.

11. V.Bl.d.W.-SS., Nr.18, 15 September 1943, Ziff.334.

12. Ibid., Nr.16, 15 August 1944, Ziff.482.

13. Since 1 July 1942, members of the Kraftfahrtechnische Lehranstalt also wore orange. Ibid., Nr.13, 1 July 1942, Ziff.232.

## AUSRÜSTUNG

Equipment

For the purpose of this book, personal equipment has been defined as standard equipment issued to a soldier on entering the Waffen-SS, and kept on charge by him throughout his service. To avoid unnecessary repetition the following descriptions generally apply to materials used in the manufacture of standard German issue personal equipment.

Leather: Normally black, but brown was also used for small fittings, straps, reinforcing and linings.

Webbing: Either field-grey, olive green, or light khaki (sand colour) in various widths. Towards the end of the war many different kinds of non-standard webbing were used.

Canvas: Usually olive green or field-grey, but the old pre-war black and grey canvases continued to be used throughout the war. During the last two years of the war any available canvas was used, and it is quite common to find one piece of equipment made-up from two or more different types and colours of canvas.

Stitching: This was a very distinctive feature of Second World War German equipment and was usually white. No attempt was made at manufacturing stage to stain it to match the colour of the materials sewn, since this would have impaired its durability; in any case, repeated cleaning and polishing by the wearer soon stained it.

Metal fittings: Buckles, clips, rivets, and studs were usually made of a light metal alloy or steel, mostly painted field-grey. The colour of the finish varied considerably from light to dark grey. Towards the end of the war there was an attempt to introduce a standard colour for the Waffen-SS and armed forces (previously the air-force had blue-grey fittings). This dark steel-grey colour was used on all metal fittings including metal buttons, but was introduced too late to become standard.

Mess-tins and metal cups were at first made of aluminium with a matt black finish, which usually chipped off, exposing the aluminium; they were later made of steel with an olive green enamelled finish.

Gas mask containers were painted field-grey throughout the war.

### General note

Initially all wooden and metal containers as well as ordnance and vehicles were painted field-grey; by 1943 the colour had proved impractical when used on fronts with differing terrain and dark yellow was adopted as standard basic colour.[1] Contrary to popular belief items painted in this colour were not necessarily intended for North Africa, but for all war theatres, both temperate and tropical, since it was much easier to apply a darker camouflage pattern

Duty N.C.O. (Unterführer vom Dienst) was distinguished by wearing an aluminium cord lanyard on the right shoulder. This practise which was not common in the SS.

Top to bottom: 1932 model SS officers belt buckle. 1932 model SS other ranks belt buckle. Prototype other ranks belt buckle made by Assman & Söhne and probably never produced in any quantities.

(to suit the terrain) to a light ground than vice versa. After this date all equipment left the factory finished in the standard colour.

**Feldausrüstung**

Field equipment

**Koppel**

Waist belt

The waist belt was issued to all other ranks and was worn with all orders of dress. Since it constituted a degradation to have the belt taken away whilst under arrest, those serving in penal units were issued with a strap for the bread bag if they did not already have one.[2] The only soldiers allowed out without a belt were those in military hospitals or convalescing. It was usual practice for junior officers to equip themselves with belts of other ranks from their unit's stocks for wear in the field, but this was discontinued in July 1943 because of shortages.[3]

The leather belt was $4\frac{1}{2}$ cm wide with a metal hook at one end and a leather tongue with two rows of holes on the reverse of the other end, to which the buckle was attached and adjusted. Belts with a lacquered finish were not officially allowed. Webbing belts do not appear to have been generally issued to Waffen-SS personnel.

**Koppelschloss**

Belt buckle

The standard rectangular SS belt buckle was originally introduced in 1932.[4] Before the war the buckle was usually made of nickel plated steel, and later in an alloy with a matt silver (aluminium) finish. During the war the issue belt buckle was painted field-grey.

**Seitengewehr**

Bayonet

During the Second World War the final pattern of 84/98 bayonet was standard issue. It had wooden grips and had originally been issued to mounted troops in 1915. Just before the war bakelite grips began to replace the wooden ones, but in 1944-45 wooden grips began to be used again. During the war only those issued with a rifle received a bayonet, and when German bayonets were not available foreign ones were issued. When no bayonet was available the frog was worn empty.

**Seitengewehrtasche**

Bayonet frog

The bayonet was carried in a black leather frog (20 × 5 cm) worn on the left hip suspended from the waist belt. The standard frog was produced in two patterns — the cavalry version, as opposed to the infantry one, had a narrow leather strap which held the grip of the bayonet to prevent it swinging violently. With the introduction of the folding entrenching tool, a new bayonet frog (19 x 3 cm) was introduced. In November 1942 restrictions were imposed on the wearing of bayonets and frogs by personnel employed in offices or Ersatz units on Reich territory. [5]

## Patronentaschen
Ammunition pouches

**98K.** These ammunition pouches were made of leather ($9\frac{1}{2}$ x 19 x 3 cm) and were designed to take 30 rounds in six clips (two clips to a compartment). Most personnel in field units were issued with two pouches, but those with a small ammunition requirement, such as artillerymen, received one. This pouch pattern had also been issued to mounted personnel in 1915, remaining virtually unchanged until the end of the Second World War, although increasing use was made of rivets to replace stitching. In June 1942 troops were advised to modify their pouches by adding a small strip of leather to the top to prevent clips from falling out when it was left open. [6]

**MP 28.** Those equipped with this sub machine-gun were issued with a black leather pouch for three magazines, which had a large flap covering the front.

**MP 38 & 40.** This was a canvas pouch (23 x 15 cm) designed to take three magazines, and was normally issued in pairs. The left pouch was fitted with a small pocket at the base of the left magazine container, which was designed to hold the loading tool.

**G41, G41(W) & G43.** This pouch with two compartments was designed to take two magazines of the first German automatic rifle which was issued in limited quantities. The pouch was made of a synthetic rubberised fabric with leather and metal fittings. [7]

**MP43, MP43/1, MP44 & StG44.** New pouches were designed to take the long slightly curved magazine of the automatic assault rifle. The canvas pouch (25 x 20 x $3\frac{1}{2}$ cm) held three magazines, and were made and issued in pairs, which were joined together by a narrow webbing strap to prevent heavily laden pouches from falling forwards. Both pouches had small pockets for stripping tools and accessories. These pouches were manufactured from the poorest materials, canvas, odd bits of rubber, and other synthetic fabrics.

## Gasmaske und Tragbüchse
Gas mask and container

The standard German army gas mask was carried in a 250 mm-long cylindrical metal container which was carried as follows: [8]

Unmounted personnel wore it suspended from the right hip from a strap over the left shoulder. When this was not practical, for instance by light machine-gunners or by complete units, then it could be worn on the left hip with the strap over the right shoulder.

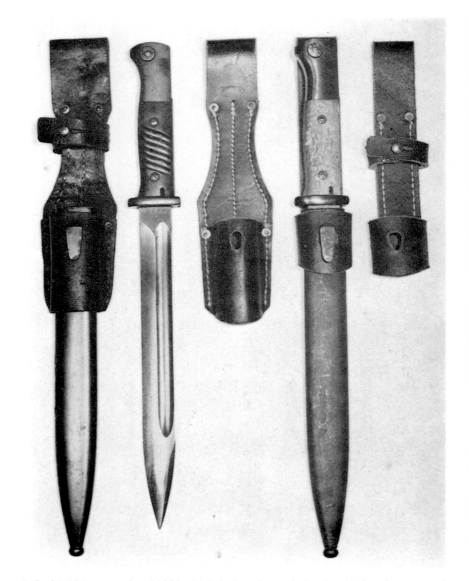

L-R: 84/98 bayonet dated 1939 with bakelite grips and sheath with frog for mounted personnel. Standard frog for unmounted personnel. 84/98 bayonet dated 1944 with wooden grips and matt finished sheath and frog for use in conjunction with the folding entrenching tool. Final pattern frog for mounted personnel.

Waffen-SS man carrying the 1st World War long-barrelled Mauser in its butt-holster and field glasses in their case. The helmets have been daubed with mud for camouflage, France 1940.

Mounted personnel, as above, but more to the front with the waist belt over the container carrying straps to prevent it flapping violently.

Drivers of motor vehicles including motor-cyclists wore it on the breast at elbow level, with the lid towards the right.

In 1939 the container dimensions were slightly altered. The length was increased to 275 mm, and the diameter reduced from 120½–120 mm. Field units were uniformly equipped with the new pattern. Those issued with a gas mask were expected to carry it at all times when being posted, transferred, or when travelling.

**Gasplane**

Gas cape

The anti-gas cape was carried in a canvas pouch (17 x 23 cm), and was either attached to the gas mask container strap and worn on the chest, or strapped to the container itself. Later in the war the cape was rarely worn.

**Kleines Schanzzeug**

Entrenching tool

The entrenching tool consisted of a 15 cm-wide flat or pointed steel blade on a straight wooden handle (overall length 55 cm). It was carried in a leather or canvas case (Tasche) suspended from the waist belt on the left hip. The shovel was kept in place by a strap which encompassed both handle and bayonet sheath when worn together.

In 1942 a folding entrenching tool (Zusammenklappbares Schanzzeug) measuring 69 cm-long extended and 49 cm folded, was introduced. By means of a Bakelite nut the pointed steel blade could be locked in any one of three positions — in line with the handle as a shovel, at right angles to the handle as a pick, or folded against the handle for carrying. A special leather and metal case with single belt loop (and one for bayonet sheath) was issued with it. This new case made it necessary to re-design the bayonet frog; it also provided a useful means of carrying the stick grenade.

**Zeltbahn und Zubehör**

Groundsheet and accessories

At the beginning of the war there were four types of groundsheet used by the Waffen-SS.[10] These were the square grey 1931 model, the grey army, and camouflaged triangular army and SS patterns. By the 27 January 1939 8,400 triangular SS camouflage ones had been issued. The triangular ground-sheet measured 203 x 203 x 203 cm, and apart from its primary purpose as a portable shelter could also be worn as a cape or poncho in wet weather. There were three different methods of wearing it — for those on foot or mounted on horseback, motor-cycle, or bicycle. Normally four groundsheets could be buttoned together to form a four-man tent. although any number from one upwards could be used. In addition to the groundsheet, each soldier carried rolled inside the sheet, three 26 cm-long metal pegs, three $36\frac{1}{2}$ cm-long poles which fitted together, and a length of cord.

The groundsheet was worn in a number of different ways:

1. Rolled and tied with two $54 \times 1\frac{3}{4}$ cm-long leather or webbing straps suspended from the waist belt at the back.
2. Rolled lengthways and placed on top of the blanket and/or greatcoat, and strapped to the pack by three straps.
3. Rolled lengthways and strapped around the mess-tin to form an assault pack.
4. Rolled and strapped on top of the canvas pouch of the assault pack with the two straps provided.
5. Rolled and strapped to the two D-rings on the back of the supporting straps.

In December 1943 it was decided not to issue groundsheet and accessory replacements to the eastern front for economy reasons; again in September 1944 there were no replacements to supply troops and crews (except to medical companies). Mounted units were equipped with only 25% of those required by supply troops and crews.[11]

### Brotbeutel
Haversack

The 1934 model bread bag (22 x 26 x 9 cm) was made of canvas with either leather or webbing and metal fittings. The flap was fastened by straps and buttons; on later models straps were dispensed with and the flap provided with two button-holes. It could be worn on the right hip suspended from the waist belt, or over the shoulder from a 3 cm-wide detachable and adjustable canvas strap. The haversack was supposed to contain washing kit, eating implements, field cap and rifle cleaning kit.

### Feldflasche (Labe-flasche) und Trinkbecher
Water-bottle and drinking cup

The water-bottle was carried on the right hip, suspended by a spring-loaded clip from a D-ring on the haversack. Its capacity was 1 litre, and was at first made of aluminium with screw cap, then plastic impregnated wood, and finally enamelled steel, with a cover of grey felt. The cup was initially made of aluminium, painted black, then field-grey enamelled steel; black plastic cups were also issued. The cup fitted over the top of the screw cap, held in place by a leather strap. The 1 litre bottle measured 25 x 16 x 8 cm, but mountain troops and medical orderlies were issued with a larger capacity bottle which was fitted with a special strap so that it could be carried over the shoulder.

### Kochgeschirr
Mess-tin

Like the water-bottle it was first made of aluminium, and towards the end of

Waffen-SS man with the leather pouch for MP 28 magazines.

SS grenadiers equipped with the assault rifle wearing the special canvas pouches designed to carry the long curved magazine, France December 1944.

Haversack (Brotbeutel) with some of its typical contents including field cap, fat container, rifle cleaning kit, sewing kit, knife, fork, spoon and Esbit cooker.

the war enamelled steel. It consisted of a shallow lid with handle, which when inverted could be used as a plate or cup. The pot was deep and fitted with a wire handle. The mess-tin measured 15 x 16 x 9 cm.

It could be carried in a number of different ways:

1. Inside the pack.
2. Strapped to the flap of the 1934 model pack.
3. Strapped to the assault pack frame.
4. Inside the flap of the engineer's assault pack.
5. Suspended by a leather strap and spring-loaded clip from the left D-ring on the haversack, alongside the water-bottle.
6. In or on the left saddle-bag.

## Koppeltraggestell
### Straps supporting
The straps supporting were designed to support both the weight of the waist belt, ammunition pouches, etc., and carry the pack, and on the M.34 pack the straps were an integral part of it. This had obvious disadvantages since the pack was never carried in action, and in 1939 a new pack was introduced which was designed to clip onto separate straps supporting. The new pattern consisted of two 59 cm-long side straps (4 cm wide reducing to $2\frac{1}{2}$ cm at their narrowest), and one 39 cm-long back strap ($2\frac{1}{2}$–2 cm wide). At the back there were two D-rings on the shoulders, from which various kinds of pack or rucksack could be suspended.

The SS were the first to experiment with lightweight webbing equipment, and as early as 1939 had a separate webbing strap supporting. At the beginning of the war the Allgemeine-SS strap supporting for mounted personnel was issued to field units of the Waffen-SS.

## Tornister
### Pack
The 1934 model pack had integral carrying straps, and was made of canvas with leather and metal fittings, and cow skin flap. It was issued with three greatcoat straps (54 x $1\frac{3}{4}$ cm).

In 1939 a new pack was introduced, which was basically the same as the 1934 model, but instead of carrying straps had two D-clips, which were designed to clip onto the D-rings on the new straps supporting. During the war some packs were produced in plain canvas, without fur covered flaps. The flap of the pack was normally used for carrying washing and sewing kit, underwear, and a handkerchief. In the pack itself were mess-tin, ankle boots, tent line, iron rations, and rifle cleaning kit. The groundsheet, and sometimes the blanket, were folded and placed between the pack and flap, the greatcoat was rolled and strapped to the top and two sides of the pack. The groundsheet was also rolled and placed on top of the greatcoat.[12]

Estonian volunteers wearing rush green drill uniforms, webbing straps supporting. The harness used to hold camouflage material is made from a haversack strap.

The assault pack with rolled blanket, mess-tin and groundsheet strapped to the iron ration bag, which was one of the many ways in which it was used in the field, July 1944.

## Sturmgepäck

### Assault pack

The assault pack was made of 4 cm-wide webbing and measured 28 x 26 cm. Attached to it were two 35 cm-long straps designed to hold the groundsheet. Detachable from the frame was a canvas bag (13 x 28 x 8½ cm) designed to hold the rifle cleaning kit in the flap, and a tent line, pullover, and reduced iron ration (tinned meat and Zwieback) in the bag. The rolled groundsheet was strapped on top.[13]

## Bekleidungssack

### Clothing bag

This canvas satchel with leather and metal fittings was issued to both mounted and unmounted troops in addition to the M.39 pack, so that each man received one pack or rucksack and clothing bag. Those units who according to the KAN were issued with two clothing bags did not receive a pack or rucksack.[14] It carried drill uniform, underpants, pair of socks, collar liner, and other miscellaneous requirements. Mounted personnel carried in addition a pair of ankle boots, razor, cleaning and sewing kit, and a pair of bathing trunks.[15] In 1944 the whole question of packs was reviewed and simplified as follows:

### 662. The equipping of officers, N.C.O.s and men with packs.

1. In view of previous experience, officers N.C.O.s and men will be issued with packs as follows:

   (a) SS officers up to and including SS-Staf.
   Large rucksack (standard rucksack)                    Art. No. 10151
   with carrying straps for unmounted
   personnel                                             Art. No. 10131

   (b) SS N.C.O.s and men
   Battle rucksack with                                  Art. No. 10152
   carrying straps for unmounted
   personnel                                             Art. No. 10131

   (c) Members of mountain units equipped with
   special mountain clothing
   Rucksack for mountain troops, small                   Art. No. 10155
   Rucksack for mountain troops, large                   Art. No. 10156

In any case it is not permitted to take other articles of luggage, such as trunks, suit-cases, clothing bags, packs, etc., other than the packs mentioned under a, b, and c above.

2. The following are rendered obsolete by this new regulation:
   Pack M.39                                             Art. No. 10132
      and assault pack to pack M.39                      Art. No. 10133
   Assault pack bag                                      Art. No. 10134

| | |
|---|---|
| Assault pack for engineers | Art. No. 10137 |
| Side pouches for engineers | Art. No. 10138 |
| Rucksack for artillery | Art. No. 10159 |
| Clothing bag | Art. No. 10160 |
| Saddle-bags for mounted personnel | — |

These items are to be worn out.

But special attention is to be paid to the fact that these items of equipment do not remain with the men as additional luggage . (See Ziff.1, 1.Abs.).

3. The quantity and type of items rendered obsolete, and surplus are to be reported at once to the SS-WVHA-Amt BII-(Feldeinheiten) or SS-FHA – Amt VI-(Ers-Einheiten) and offices in Reich territory, saddle bags to SS-FHA.Ab Ib.

4. Regarding the cancellation of saddle-bags for mounted troops, special attention is drawn to the order in the Heerestechnisches Verordnungs-blatt, 2.Jahr.14 Ausgabe of 15 July 1944, Ziff.413, which where applicable is relevant to the Waffen-SS.

SS-FHA Ia-IVa

## Mannschaftsdecke
Blanket

The issue blanket was grey with two wide and six narrow stripes at both ends. It was normally carried either inside the pack or rolled and strapped on the outside, sometimes rolled and carried over the shoulder. In November 1944 it was ordered that between 15 November 1944 and 15 March 1945 all SS members posted to field units in the east should be issued with a second blanket, in addition to the blanket included in the issue schedule(K) of the Waffen-SS.

## Meldekartentasche
Map or dispatch case

Made of leather (27 x 19 cm) it was issued to about 50% of the complete strength of a unit as laid down in the KAN.[16] It was mainly worn suspended by two adjustable straps from the waist belt by dispatch-riders and section and troop leaders. Better quality privately purchased map cases in black or brown leather were used by staff and artillery officers.

## Dienstfernglas
Service binoculars

Binoculars (6 x 30 or 10 x 50) were issued to officers and N.C.O.s, and although supplied with either a leather or Bakelite case, they were usually worn exposed round the neck, and the lenses protected by a cover. The case was designed to be worn from either the belt or carrying strap. Large numbers of more powerful private or 'booty' binoculars were also used.

Norwegian volunteers wearing the pack with rolled blanket and groundsheet and empty bayonet frog The soldier on the right has a clothing bag.

Typical Waffen-SS men during a pause in the battle for France, 1940. This clearly shows the gas cape pouch and issue field glasses, as well as an interesting selection of neckerchiefs.

## MG-Werkzeugtasche
Machine-gun tool and accessory case
Carried by machine-gunners instead of the right ammunition pouch, (the left pouch was replaced by a pistol holster) it measured 19 x 16 x 16 cm and contained tools, cleaning kit, spare bolt, length of ammunition belt, and an anti-aircraft sight. Attached to the front of the pouch was a piece of heat resistant cloth for use when changing a hot barrel.

## MG-Laufbehälter
MG barrel container
A 65 cm-long cylindrical metal container for carrying a spare barrel for the MG 42. Two versions existed – for single or twin barrels. The strap was adjustable and made of webbing with metal fittings.

## Handgranatensack
Hand-grenade bag
Introduced in 1939 for assault troop use, and based on the type used in the First World War, it consisted of two bags (38 x 18 cm) joined at the top and bottom corners by webbing straps. The bags hung round the neck on either side of the body, and were held in place by an adjustable strap around the wearer's back. Each bag held 3 stick grenades (Stielhangranate 24) and was fastened at the top with a zip-fastener.

## Schleppriemen
Sling
A wide black leather or canvas adjustable strap which was worn over the left shoulder. At the end of the sling was a large metal spring-loaded clip which was fastened to an infantry or anti-tank gun for manhandling.

### Notes:
1. Kraftfahrtechnischer Anhang zu den V.Bl.d.W.-SS, 1943, Blatt 23, Ziff.42. Anstrich des Heeresgerätes.
2. AHM. 1943, Nr.591.
3. Ibid. Nr.630.
4. V.Bl.d.OSAF. Nr.6, 26 January 1932, Ziff.22.
5. V.Bl.d.W.-SS, Nr.21, 1 November 1942, Ziff.380.
6. H.V.Bl.Teil B, Blatt 12, Ziff.505 vom 27 June 1942. V.Bl.d.W.-SS. Nr.16, 16 August 1942, Ziff.285.
7. Militaria, Vol. 1, No. 1, p. 14 with illustrations.
8. Der Dienstunterricht im Heere (Ausg. f. den Nachr.-Soldaten) pp. 135-7.
9. AHM. 1942, Nr.414.
10. V.Bl.d.W.-SS. Nr.14, 1 December 1940, Ziff.420.
11. Ibid. Nr.18, 15 September 1944, Ziff.530.
12. Der Dienstunterricht im Heere, pp. 73-5 with illustration.
13. Ibid.
14. V.Bl.d.W.-SS. Nr.16, 15 August 1942, Ziff.284.
15. Der Dienstunterricht im Heere, pp. 73-5 with illustration.
16. V.Bl.d.W.-SS. Nr.21, 1 November 1944, Ziff.660.
17. Ibid. Nr.16, 15 August 1944, Ziff.286.

**Pistolentaschen**
Pistol holsters
Holsters were usually purchased or issued with the pistol, and as such they come under the category of weapons and their accessories. They have been included here because they contributed to the external appearance of the SS soldier.

The service pistols of the Waffen-SS were the 9 mm Parabellum (Pistole 08) and the Walther (Pistole 38), although at the beginning of the war large numbers of obsolete pistols such as the long barrelled Mauser with butt-holster and captured Czech and Polish service pistols were still in use. The pistols were usually carried on the left hip, barrel facing to the back, in a black leather holster. The P.08 and early P.38 holsters were made of blocked leather, but the later P.38 was of unblocked design.

Issue holsters were usually marked as follows : P.38 jhg 1944. In this case P.38 stood for the type of pistol, jhg was the manufacturer's code, and 1944 the year of manufacture.

Officers were expected to purchase their own pistols (Eigentumswaffe) from the SS Clothing Counter against presentation of a voucher. Details of the pistol were then to be entered in the owner's pay book (Soldbuch). SS-Standartenoberjunker, who had to kit themselves, were to get pistols from their school, which was to indent on the SS-FHA, Ib for the required number. N.C.O.s were not allowed to buy pistols later in the war because of shortages. The standard officer's pistol was the Walther 7.65 mm automatic.[1]

### 1. Methods of wearing the pistol.[2]
The Reichsführer-SS has ordered that:
1. On home territory the pistol will be worn on the right, facing to the back.
2. In the operational zone, with the exception of 1 above, on manoeuvres on home territory, the pistol is to be worn according to army regulations. If these are not obtainable then the most practical method must be adopted.                                                    SS-FHA./Ia

In October 1944 officers were ordered to carry loaded pistols in public, but reminded not to leave them in cloakrooms and be careful that they were not stolen when frequenting crowded places (stations, dance-halls, etc.) or when using public transport.[3]

**Notes:**
1. V.Bl.d.W.-SS., Nr.13, 1 July 1944, Ziff.351.
2. Ibid. Nr.1, 1 January 1943, Ziff.1.
3. Ibid. Nr.19, 1 October 1944, Ziff.577.

SS grenadier with grenade bags.

117

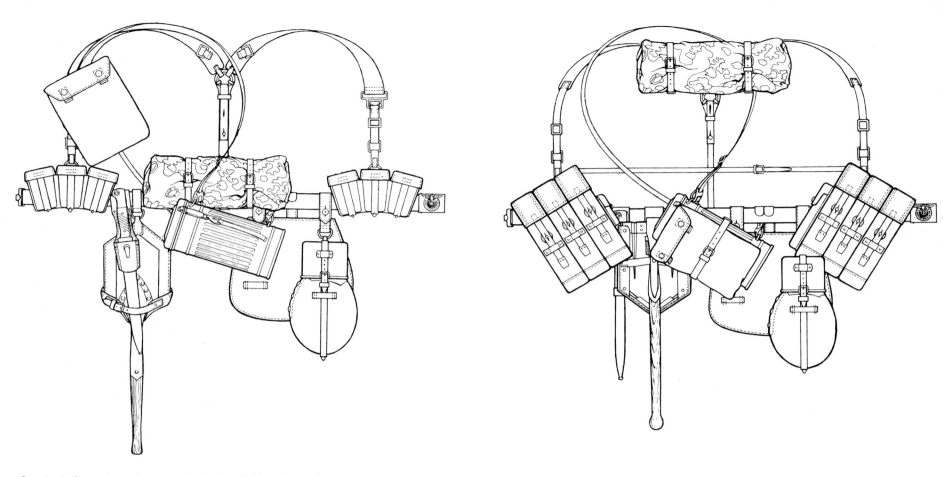

Standard rifleman's equipment at beginning (left) and end of the war.

### Führer-Leibriemen
#### Officer's belt
A 4½ cm-wide black leather belt with a white metal eye at one end and a leather tongue on the reverse of the other, with two rows of holes to allow for adjustment of the buckle. The circular buckle was of white metal alloy with either a matt silver (aluminium), or matt grey finish,* and on either side was a black leather slide. Better quality belts were usually lined on the inside with cloth; a lacquered finish was not permitted. Although the officer's belt with circular buckle continued to be worn until the end of the war it was found to be impractical. In action the belt buckle tended to come undone, so many officers adopted the belt and buckle (or belt with rectangular two pronged buckle) as worn by other ranks.

### Schulterriemen
#### Cross strap
A 2½ cm-wide black leather adjustable cross strap with white metal rectangular slide buckle and two spring-loaded white metal clips, one at each end. It was worn clipped to a D-ring slide on the left front of the waist belt, passed over the right shoulder (under the shoulder strap) and attached to a D-ring on the reverse of the belt at the back. The May 1940 order concerning the field-grey uniform abolished the wearing of the cross strap by members of the Waffen-SS with the field-grey uniform.[1]

### Feldbinde
#### Full-dress belt
In 1938 a full-dress belt (see Vol. 3, p. 79 of this series) was introduced for SS officers to wear with parade dress (Paradeanzug). It continued to be worn for the first three years of the war, its use was then restricted at about the same time as the SS sword.

## VARIATIONS ON STANDARD EQUIPMENT
### 1. Cavalry.
#### Koppeltraggestell für Berittene
Straps supporting for mounted personnel
Mounted personnel did not carry a pack, and so needed different straps supporting to carry the weight of the waist belt with its heavy load. They

*This buckle and the version worn by other ranks was introduced in 1932. In January 1937, in reply to a proposal to introduce a new pattern, Himmler wrote, 'that the question of the alteration of the SS buckle designed by the Führer himself and made from his own sketches, has never arisen'.[2]

### Notes:
1. See Appendix II.
2. Der RF-SS Tgb.Nr.A/44/H/37. Betr. Neue Entwürfe für SS-Führer-Leibriemenschlösser, Berlin, den 3 January 1937.

Medical orderly from a mounted unit with first aid pouches, Russia 1942.

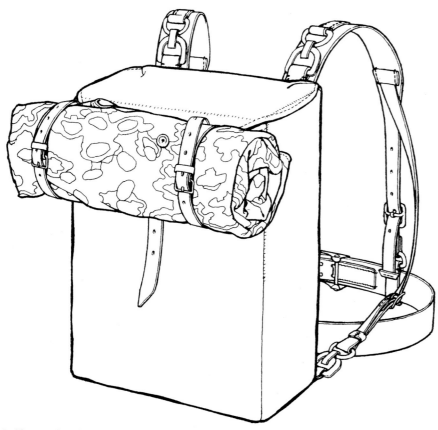

Artillery rucksack with rolled groundsheet.

therefore were issued with a simple three-piece adjustable straps supporting which was clipped to the pouches in front and to the waist belt at the back. The pre-war RZM pattern Allgemeine-SS cavalry pattern was also issued at the beginning of the war.

**Packtasche 34**[1]

Saddle-bags, model 1934

The marching pack for mounted personnel (including mounted drivers) consisted of a brown leather cavalryman and horse pack, which together made up the saddle-bag 34. The right pack (Reitergepäck) contained a pair of shoes, cleaning brush, shirt and socks, Zwieback in bag, tin of meat, sewing bag, cleaning kit washing things, and rifle cleaning kit. The left pack (Pferdegepäck) contained grooming brush, mess-tin, curry comb and surcingle. Attached to the horse pack was a pocket for two horse-shoes, 16 nails, stud spanner and 8 studs, and a tethering ring.

In addition there was a baggage case (Hintergepäck) attached to the back of the saddle containing groundsheet, corn sack with cords, canvas bucket, horse gas mask, and a greatcoat for winter. The right saddle-bag was so designed that it could also be worn on the back as a pack, to which the greatcoat could be strapped. Saddle-bags were also used on the eastern front by motor-cyclists who attached them to the front fork of their machines and used them as additional (and very necessary) stowage space. In November 1944 the saddle-bags were rendered obsolete but were to be worn out.

**2. Artillery**

Members of horse drawn artillery battalions wore the personal equipment laid down for mounted personnel.

**Rucksack für Artillerie**

Artillery rucksack

In January 1943 a new canvas rucksack (36 x 26 x 11 cm) was introduced for artillerymen, designed to be worn both as a pack and assault pack. Many variations of this rucksack existed. The top of the rucksack was fastened by a draw-string and buckled flap. On the front were two 54 cm-long straps for the rolled groundsheet. Some rucksacks had integral adjustable carrying straps, others had separate straps. According to the army introduction order the infantry straps supporting was not to be used with this rucksack.[2]

**3. Engineers.**

Engineers wore the same standard equipment as other foot personnel, but because of their special tasks carried additional items of equipment, such as demolition charges and detonators, shovels, and matchetes. In 1941 the army introduced the engineer's assault pack,[3] which was immediately adopted by the Waffen-SS. It consisted of the following:

Straps supporting for unmounted personnel.                    Art. No. 127

Pack M.39.                                     Art. No. 302
Back pack for engineers.                        Art. No. 331
2 side pouches for engineers.                    Art. No. 332

The back pack and side pouches were issued to every fifth assault engineer. The back pack was suspended from the standard strap supporting, and contained at the bottom a 3 Kg demolition charge, and above, two smoke pots. In the flap there was a special pouch for the mess-tin. The side pouches were worn in place of the ammunition pouches and came in pairs, left and right. Both pouches held egg shaped grenades, but the right pouch had a special pocket for the gas mask without container. Rifle ammunition in clips was held in individual pouches. [4]

### 4. Mountain troops.

For list of standard equipment for mountain troops, see list in section dealing with mountain troop uniform. The basic difference between mountain troops and other infantry units was that they were issued with a rucksack instead of a pack and a larger capacity water-bottle, with carrying strap.

Climbing equipment consisted of Manila rope in 100-foot lengths, ice axe, crampons, pitons, snaplinks, steel-edged mountain skis, and small oval snow-shoes. Additional specialised equipment was issued as and when required for rescue work. [5]

### 5. Bicycle squadrons.

Personnel in bicycle squadrons (Radfahrschwadronen) were initially issued with the infantry straps supporting, assault pack, and clothing bag, but in January 1943 the Waffen-SS followed the army lead and issued them with the artillery rucksack and a clothing bag. [6]

### 6. Medical personnel. [7]

Unmounted medical orderlies carried two 17 x 10 x 8 cm black leather pouches (Sanitätstaschen) instead of ammunition pouches. They carried various first-aid equipment, field dressings, etc. Mounted orderlies carried a pouch which could be attached to the saddle, but during the war they also wore the pouches for unmounted orderlies. A larger 2 litre water-bottle (Labeflasche) and carrying strap was used by both orderlies and stretcher-bearers. Larger quantities of urgently needed dressings, etc., could also be carried in the medical pack (Sanitätstornister), which was basically the same as the standard pack, but had a white circle with red cross on the flap. Doctors, dentists, and chemists carried special equipment in a black leather case with carrying strap :

| | | |
|---|---|---|
| Doctors | Arzttasche | (Heeres-Modell) |
| | | (SS-Modell 34) |
| Dentists | Zahnarzttasche. | |
| Chemists | Apothekertasche. | |

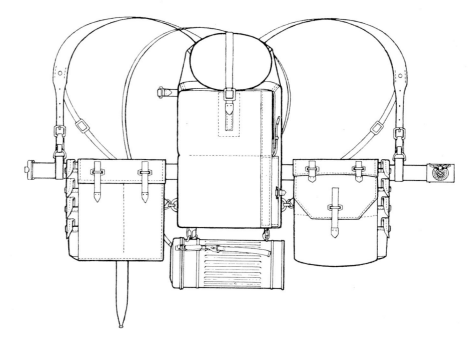

Engineer's assault pack.

SS-Obersturmführer Hempel, 1st Company SS-Wach-Bataillon Böhmen-Mähren spring 1941, wearing the old pattern SS sabre with officer's knot.

**Notes:**

1. Der Dienstunterricht im Heere. pp. 73-5 with illustrations.
2. V.Bl.d.W.-SS. Nr.2, 15 January 1943, Ziff. 28.
   H.V.Bl.16. Ausgabe. Berlin den 7 July 1942, Ziff.1000.
3. V.Bl.d.W.-SS. Nr.20, 1 November 1941, Ziff. 446.
4. Handbook on German Military Forces, 15 March 1945, p. IX-25.
5. Ibid.
6. V.Bl.d.W.-SS. Nr.2, 15 January 1943, Ziff.29.
7. Sanitäts-Vorschrift für die Allgemeine-SS (SS-San.-V.) (SS-Dv. Nr.8) Tegernsee, den 16 August 1935.

## SS-SEITENWAFFEN

SS Side arms

At the beginning of the war Waffen-SS officers wore either the SS sword (Degen) or the army pattern sabre with white metal fittings, which although obsolete continued to be worn. (For details of the introduction and award of the SS sword, and method of wearing, see Vol. 3, pp. 70-4).

On 18 December 1939 the wearing of the SS sword by members of the SS was forbidden for the duration of the war,[1] but on 1 April 1940 this order was rescinded and the sword was allowed to be worn by those officers entitled to it, when not on field or training duty.[2] In August 1940 it was announced that swords would no longer be available to N.C.O:s on promotion to SS-Oberscharführer, but those with swords could continue to wear them.[3]

In August 1942 the wearing of the sword was again restricted:

### 280. Wearing of the sword forbidden.[4]

The Reichsführer-SS has, for the duration of the war, forbidden the wearing of the sword by officers and N.C.O.s, on or off duty.

Colour escorts, guards of honour, guard mounting detachments, as well as those taking part in oath taking ceremonies are excepted.

The Reichsführer-SS will authorise certain exceptions from time to time.

Kdo.d.W.-SS/Ia

In February 1943 the Reichsführer-SS authorised the wearing of the SS Service Dagger 36 (Modell 1936) by Waffen-SS officers with long trousers.*

*On 16 September 1941 SS-Gruf. Pohl submitted a prototype dagger, with hanger, portepee, and case, together with a further three designs for an SS dagger for the Waffen-SS. There is no record of any written reaction from Himmler, although the accompanying letter bears a note in pencil 'after the war'.[6] In reply to a prototype submitted by SS-Ogruf. Weitzel, Himmler postponed any decision until after the war.[7]

## 64. Wearing of the SS Service Dagger 36 with portepee. [5]

The Reichsführer-SS has, for the duration of the war, authorised the wearing of the SS Service Dagger 36 with the army portepee by Waffen-SS officers.

The dagger may be worn with all orders of dress not requiring a waist belt.

SS-FHA./Amt II/Ia

### Kampfmesser
Fighting knife

The personal knife has always been an essential item of a soldier's equipment, not only for fighting, but for the more mundane activities of life in the field. During the First World War various semi-official patterns of knife were manufactured in large quantities and issued to troops fighting at the front. During the latter stages of the Second World War, fighting knives, based on those used in the First World War, were again issued to front-line personnel for close-quarter fighting. Although many issue and private types co-existed, the issue pattern predominated.

The knife was made of steel (overall length 30 cm, blade 17 cm) with beech wood grip and stamped metal scabbard with black enamel finish. On the reverse of the scabbard was a spring steel clip. The knife could be worn in a number of different ways, but in action the most typical was inside the boot or clipped to the front of the field blouse or camouflage smock at chest level.

### Notes:

1. Der RF-SS (i.V. SS-Ogruf. Heissmeyer) SS-Befehl, Berlin den 18 December 1939.

2. V.B. Insp. (E) SS-VT, Nr.1., 1 April 1940.

3. V.Bl.d.W.-SS. Nr. 6, 15 August 1940.

4. Ibid. Nr.16, 15 August 1943, Ziff.280.

5. Ibid., Nr.4, 15 February 1943, Ziff.64 and Nr.10, 15 May 1943, Ziff.182 with illustration showing correct method of attaching the knot.

6. Der Chef des Hauptamtes Haushalt u.Bauten, SS-Gruf. Pohl I/3 1751 Ri/Gu. Betr.: SS-Dolch für die Waffen-SS. Anlg.: 1 SS-Dolch mit Gehänge und Portepee in Etui, 1 SS-Dolch neue Ausführung, 3 Entwürfe (Zeichnungen), Berlin Lichterfelde-West, den 16 September 1941.

7. RF-SS (Ru/Gr.) an HSSPF Nord SS-Ogruf. Weitzel, June 1940.

Officer in walking out dress with the 1936 Model SS service dagger with knot.

SS grenadier during the Ardennes Offensive armed with a fighting knife and captured Colt automatic pistol, December 1944.

One of the most common patterns of the combat knife, showing both the obverse and reverse of the sheath.

# APPENDIX I

Berlin, den 12 December 1939
Der Reichsführer-SS und Chef der Deutschen Polizei im Reichsministerium des Innern-Hauptamt Haushalt und Bauten-I/3 009.

### SS Order

Re.: The field-grey uniform of the Waffen-SS

Many uncertainties exist concerning the field-grey uniform of the Waffen-SS, and so I hereby order the following:

1. **Blouse:**
   (a) **N.C.O.s and men:** The field blouse is manufactured in the same cut as that of the army, with dark green badge cloth collar, button-on liner, and pleated pockets. The blouse is to be worn open with brown shirt and black tie. The blouse may be worn closed by order of the commander, on training, exercises, and special duties.
   (b) **Officers:** The officer's field blouse is the same cut as that of the men, and is also worn open with brown shirt and black tie. It may be worn closed only when the men have theirs closed. The wearing of field blouses with stand-and-fall collar (army officers' field blouses) is forbidden.

2. **Greatcoat:**
   The greatcoat retains its existing cut. The collar will be made from dark green badge cloth.

3. **Tunic (Rock):**
   Officers may also wear the tunic. The cut is the same as that of the black service tunic. The collar is the same colour as the rest of the tunic, and not dark green. The commander will specify on each occasion whether the field blouse or tunic is to be worn, so that the officers' corps is uniformly dressed.

4. **Trousers:**
   (a) **Officers:** Officers are allowed, as from now, to wear long field-grey trousers on duty, when their men are wearing long trousers and ankle boots.
   (b) **N.C.O.s and men:** Generally only long field-grey trousers will be issued; only mounted personnel will be issued with riding breeches. Troops may continue to wear other existing patterns without alteration.
   Non-regulation items of clothing may be worn by officers until 1 April 1940.

5. **Field-grey head-dress:**
   (a) **Officers:** Field-grey service caps with black velvet band and black peak (Vulkanfibre) are to be worn with field-grey uniform. With immediate effect a field cap (Schiffchenmütze) in field-grey trikot, identical in cut to the air-force officer's model is to be worn. On it is to be sewn an aluminium embroidered national emblem and death's head. Officers have until 1 January 1940 to equip themselves with the new field cap.
   (b) **Senior N.C.O.s (Portepee-Unterführer):** Field-grey service cap with black band, peak, and leather chin-strap will be worn inside the barracks. On all other occasions when the steel helmet is not specified they will wear the other ranks' field cap.
   (c) **N.C.O.s and men:** On all occasions when the steel helmet is not specified, the field cap must be worn. When with their men, N.C.O.s may wear the old model peaked field cap.

6. **Shoulder straps and metal insignia for officers:**
   (a) Without exception the shoulder straps of the armed forces (Wehrmacht) in matt aluminium will be worn on the field blouse tunic, and greatcoat. The wearing of bright aluminium braid on the shoulder straps is hereby forbidden. The colour of the underlay, for all officers in all units, is black (the SS colour). In addition the army branch of service colour (Waffenfarbe) will be worn as piping. Executive regulations are hereby decreed by the Chief of the Hauptamt Haushalt und Bauten in agreement with the Inspectorate of the SS-Verfügungstruppe and the Leader of the SS-Totenkopfverbände.
   Officers in the administrative and medical services, etc., will for the time being wear the Waffenfarbe of the unit to which they are attached. The wearing of special badges on the shoulder straps, such as the Aesculapiuss rod and the letter V (Verwaltung), or the wearing of piping in special colours by administrative officials and medical officers is forbidden. Badges of rank may only be worn if they conform to the ranks laid down by the Hauptamt für Haushalt und Bauten.
   (b) Metal badges (stars, numerals and letters) will in future be in bronzed metal.

7. **Cuff-bands:**
   Cuff-bands will be worn on the black and field-grey uniform (blouse, tunic, and greatcoat), but not on the drill uniform.

8. The Hauptamt Haushalt und Bauten will issue the necessary executive instructions for this order.

9. I wish to make it known once again, that the one and only walking-out uniform of the SS is the black uniform.

I hereby insist that commanders react strongly to contraventions of these regulations.

I also expect that from now on the variety of field-grey uniforms and insignia, which have been reported up to now, will be declared invalid, and that uniformity in the field-grey uniform, including that of the officers' corps, will be established.

Der Reichsführer-SS
gez. H. Himmler

In agreement with the Chief of the SS-Hauptamt, the following regulations are to be added to the RFSS order of 12 December 1939 HHB I/3 009.

Para. 1 (a) The old pattern field blouse and the pattern with the same colour collar are to be worn out. With the continuation of the war for a long period, a blouse with the same colour collar will again be delivered.

The order that the blouse is to be worn open with brown shirt and black tie will be disregarded for the rest of the war. Normally the blouse will be worn closed and only opened on special order.

The appendix to the order of the Hauptamt Haushalt und Bauten, Amt.KL of 11 February 1939 I/3 M 204/3 geh. is hereby amended. The 2 trikot brown shirts included in the soldiers clothing schedule are to be cancelled. Depending on stocks, either 2 white or 2 brown trikot shirts will be issued instead.

Para. 1 (b) Para. 1(a) remains unchanged. The collar must not have more than one hook and eye.

Para. 2. The greatcoat with the same colour collar is to be worn out. Alterations are not permitted.

Para. 4. The date by which non-regulation uniforms must no longer be worn has been extended to 1 July 1940.

Para. 5. The regulation field-grey officer's cap is only obtainable from the SS-Kleiderkasse, München 33.
The old N.C.O.'s peaked field cap may be worn out.

Para. 6. The branch of service colours on the shoulder strap for the field-grey uniform correspond to those laid down and introduced in the army. See attached appendix.*

Shoulder straps for N.C.O.s and men are basically made of black cloth, like those of officers.

Special regulations for the SS-Polizei-Division will follow. Officers' shoulder straps are only obtainable from the SS-Kleiderkasse, München 33.

Divisions indent for their requirement of new shoulder straps at the SS-Clothing Depot (SS-Bekleidungslager). The old pattern shoulder straps are to be returned by the divisions to the Ersatz units who will use them on their training uniform. It is up to the troop administration to comply with this.

Priority is to be given to the supply of field units.

Following the execution of the above, Ersatz units will be equipped with shoulder straps for their field uniform. The unit administration is to collectively notify their requirements according to their present strength. The delivery of new shoulder straps to the verstärkten SS-Totenkopf-Standarten and SS-Rekruten-Standarten will not take place until existing stocks have been completely used up.

The piping on the service cap and long trousers will remain white.

*This appendix has been incorporated in the chart on page 104-6. It is also the un-published order on which the SS uniform chart (see page 133) was based.

## APPENDIX II

### Copy

Der Reichsführer-SS und                                         Berlin, den 10 May 1940.
Chef der Deutschen Polizei
im Reichsministerium des Innern.

### SS Order

**Subject:** Field-grey uniform of the Waffen-SS and Security Police and SD.
**Ref.:** Order of 12 December 1939 Hauptamt Haushalt und Bauten I/3 009.
**Appendices:** 3
**Distribution:** See last page.
Further to my order of the 12 December 1939, I hereby order the following:

### I. Waffen-SS

1. The field blouse is basically the same for officers and men and is normally worn open with brown shirt and black tie.

Only in special cases (rain, storm, cold, etc.) may the blouse be worn closed over the shirt and tie. The cut of the blouse may be altered so that it can be loosely and comfortably closed over the tie.

**2.** The piping on officers' long grey trousers is not to be in Waffen-farbe, but uniformly in a grey colour.

**3.** Piping in Waffenfarbe will be worn on the service cap. Piping for officers with the rank of SS-Oberführer and above remains in aluminium.

**4.** Metal badges for officers (stars, numerals, and letters) from now on will be in bronzed metal. Gilt metal badges may be worn until 31 December 1940 at the latest.
General officers with the rank of SS-Brigadeführer and above will have silvered metal badges.

**5.** (a) Officer's shoulder straps remain in the existing pattern with black underlay.
Shoulder straps for N.C.O.s and men are also uniformly made of black cloth.
Shoulder straps will be piped in the branch of service colour (Waffenfarbe). See Appendix I.*
For members of the special services (administration, legal, technical and recruiting services and staff of the Garrison Commander) orange piping.
Members of the medical services wear cornflower blue piping.
Members of the concentration camp staff wear light brown piping.
Members of the main offices (SS-Hauptämter), that is to say those at Reich level, wear light grey piping.
Waffen-SS officers with general's rank (Brigadeführer and above) wear the underlay in the same colour as the greatcoat lapels (silver grey) without piping.

(b) Officers wear bronzed metal badges on their shoulder straps. Senior N.C.O.s wear these badges in white metal.
The badges are machine-embroidered in chain-stitch for other ranks. For the duration of the war shoulder straps will be supplied plain, and the units will be identified by a detachable slide on which is embroidered the unit badge.

(c) Since doctors in action wear the Red Cross brassard, the Aesculapius rod is to be removed from the shoulder strap.

Paragraph 6 covers cuff-bands which will be covered in Vol. 7 of the present series.

**7.** All members of the Waffen-SS (including those in SS divisions) wear their badge of rank on the left collar patch as before.
Members of the SS-T-Division and its Ersatz units, Generalinspekteur der SS-T.-St., SS-T-Standarten, Inspekteur der KL and the KL wear the death's head on its own, on the right collar patch.
All other members of the Waffen-SS wear the SS runes on their own, on the right collar patch.
Officers with the rank of SS-Standartenführer and above wear their badge of rank on both collar patches.

**8.** The entire embroidery of all insignia on the field uniform of all SS members is matt silver grey, and aluminium on the officer's tunic.

**9.** For the rest of the war, members of the Waffen-SS will not wear the leather cross strap with field-grey uniform.

**10.** All other matters are covered in my order of 12 December 1939.

Chapter II on the uniform of the SD and Security Police has been omitted.

### III. General

These regulations do not cover existing uniforms of other ranks which may continue to be worn.
Certain items of officers' clothing, which do not comply to these regulations may be worn until 31 December 1940 at the latest. The branch of service colour must be adopted immediately.
The Hauptamt Haushalt und Bauten will issue the necessary manufacturing regulations.
gez. H. Himmler.

F.d.R.d.A.
(gez.)
SS-Scharführer.

*This appendix has been incorporated in the chart on p. 104-6.

| # | Name | Region | Wi. | RA | NSK | HWL | TWL | BKL | BKW | KK | Date |
|---|------|--------|-----|----|----|----|----|----|----|----|------|
| 1. | Apeldoorn | Holland | | | | | TWL | | | | 8.43 |
| 2. | Arolsen-Waldeck | IX | | | | | | BKL | | | 44 |
| 3. | Auschwitz | VIII | | | | HWL | | | | | 44 |
| 4. | Baden-Baden | V | | | | HWL | | | | | 44 |
| 5. | Bayreuth | XIII | | | | | | | BKW | | 44 |
| 6. | Beneschau | BM | | | | | TWL | | | | |
| 7. | Bergen-Belsen | XI | | | | | | BKL | | | 44 |
| 8. | Berlin | III | | | | HWL | TWL | | | | 43/44 |
| 9. | Betscherek | Jugoslawien | | | | | | | | | |
| 10. | Bobruisk | Russ. Mitte | | | NSK | | | BKL | | | −1.44 |
| 11. | Brandenburg a.d. Havel. | III | | | NSK | | | BKL | | | 44 |
| 12. | Braunschweig | XI | | | | | TWL | BKL | | | |
| 13. | Breslau | VIII | | | | | | | | | |
| 14. | Brüssel | Belgien | | RA | | | | | | | |
| 15. | Budapest | Ungarn | | RA | | | | | | | |
| 16. | Bütow/Westpr. | II | | | | | | BKL | | | 44 |
| 17. | Dachau | VII | Wi. | | | HWL | | BKL | | | 35–45 |
| 18. | Danzig | X | Wi. | | | | | BKL | | | 44 |
| 19. | Danzig/Langfuhr | X | | | | | TWL | | | | 44 |
| 20. | Den Haag | Holland | Wi. | RA | | HWL | | | | | 7.44 |
| 21. | Dnepropetrowsk | Russ Süd | | | NSK | | | BKL | | | −1.44 |
| 22. | Frankfurt/Oder | III | | | | HWL | | | | | |
| 23. | Gotha | IX | | | | | TWL | | | | 42–44 |
| 24. | Iffezheim/Baden | V | | | | HWL | | | | | |
| 25. | Kassel/Breitenbach | IX | | | | HWL | | | | | 44 |
| 26. | Kirchheim unter Teck (Stuttgart) | V | | | | | TWL | | | | |
| 27. | Kiew | Russ. | | | | | | | | KK | |
| 28. | Krakau | GG | Wi. | | | | | | | | |
| 29. | Lemberg | GG | | | | | TWL | | | | 7.42 |
| 30. | Lieberose über Cottbus/NL. | III | | | | | | BKL | | | |
| 31. | Litzmannstadt | GG | | | | | | BKL | | | |
| 32. | Lomscha | GG | | | | | | | | | |
| 33. | Lublin | GG | | | | | | | | KK | |
| 34. | Lüneburg | X | | | | | TWL | | | | |
| 35. | Mailand | Italien | | RA | | | | | | | |
| 36. | Mainz | XII | | | | | TWL | | | | 44 |
| 37. | Merano | Italien | | | | | | BKL | | | |
| 38. | Mörchingen | XII | | | | | TWL | | | | |
| 39. | München | VII | | | | HWL | | | | | |

| No. | Location | Region | | | | | | | | |
|---|---|---|---|---|---|---|---|---|---|---|
| 40. | Opladen | VI | | | TWL | | | | | |
| 41. | Oranienburg | III | | | TWL | | BKL | BKW | | 44 |
| 42. | Oslo | Norwegen | Wi. | | TWL | | | | KK | |
| 43. | Oulu | Finnland | | NSK | | | BKL | | | |
| 44. | Paris | Frankreich | RA | | | | | | KK | |
| 45. | Paris-Villettes | Frankreich | | | TWL | | | | | |
| 46. | Poniatowa | GG | | | | | | BKW | | |
| 47. | Prag-Reuth | BM | | | TWL | | | | KK | 43 |
| 48. | Prettin/Elbe | IV | | | | | BKL | | | 44 |
| 49. | Radom-Blizyn | GG | | | | | | BKW | | |
| 50. | Rastatt | V | | | HWL | | | | | |
| 51. | Ravensbrück/Fürstenburg | II | | | | NSL | BKL | | | 40–45 |
| 52. | Reval | Estonien | | | TWL | | | | | |
| 53. | Riga | Latvien | | NSK | TWL | | BKL | | KK | 44 |
| 54. | Rowno | GG | | | | | BKL | | | |
| 55. | Sandweier | XXI | | | HWL | | | | | 4.44 |
| 56. | Schlackenwerth | XIII | | | | | BKL | | | |
| 57. | Schröttersburg | I | | | | | BKL | BKW | | 44 |
| 58. | s'Hertzogenbosch | Holland | | | TWL | | | | | 8.43 |
| 59. | Spremberg/Lausitz | III | | | | | BKL | | | 44 |
| 60. | Stettin-Stolzhagen | II | | | | | BKL | | | |
| 61. | Straubing | VII | | | | | | BKW | | 40 |
| 62. | Thorn | XX | | | TWL | | | | | 44 |
| 63. | Trawniki | GG | | | | | | BKW | | |
| 64. | Warschau | GG | | | | | BKL | | KK | 44 |
| 65. | Wehlan | I | | | TWL | | | | | 44 |
| 66. | Weimar-Buchenwald | IX | | | | NSL | | | | |
| 67. | Wien | XVII | | | | | | | | 6.44 |

**Key:**

| | | |
|---|---|---|
| BM | Böhmen-Mähren | Czechoslovakia |
| GG | General-Gouvernement | Poland |
| Wi | Wirtschaftsinspektion | Economic Inspectorate |
| RA | Rohstoffamt | Raw Material Office |
| NSK | Nachschubkommandantur | Supply Command |

| | | | |
|---|---|---|---|
| HWL | Hauptwirtschaftslager | Main Supply Depot |
| TWL | Truppenwirtschaftslager | Troop Supply Depot |
| BKL | Bekleidungslager | Clothing Depot |
| BKW | Bekleidungswerke | Clothing Works |
| KK | Kleiderkasse | Clothing Counter |

## Notes to Appendix III

1. There was also a Baumwollspinnerei at Bayreuth.

10. The Supply Command and Clothing Depot at Bobruisk (also referred to as Nachschubkommandantur der Waffen-SS und Polizei Russland-Mitte, Bobruisk-Waldlager Kisselwitschi) was evacuated to Truppübungsplatz Moorlager on 15 May 1942, and finally disbanded on 15 April 1944.

17. There was also an equipment Works (Ausrüstungswerke) at Dachau.

21. The Supply Command and Clothing Depot at Dnepropetrowsk was disbanded on 15 April 1944.

23. Iffezheim is believed to have been part of Hauptwirtschaftslager II at Rastatt in April 1944.

32. A Hauptnachschublager (Main Supply Depot) was reported at Lublin.

35. The TWL at Mainz was a branch or sub-depot (Zweigstelle).

36. The Clothing Depot or works at Merano was a sub-depot (Aussenstelle).

40. The works at Oranienburg specialised in breaking down and repairing old leather equipment (Altsachenverwertungsstelle Leder) in November 1943.

49. HWLII was originally in Berlin before being moved to Rastatt (Sandweier) in 1944. It was also reported at Iffezheim.

60. Straubing was a prison (Sicherungsanstalt) where old clothing was broken down for re-working or disposal (Instandsetzungs und Verwertungstelle).

### Mobile Clothing Maintenance Units

In addition to static clothing works and depots there were at least three mobile units whose job it was to travel from unit to unit maintaining clothing:
Bekleidungs-Instandsetzungs-Zug 500
Bekleidungs-Instandsetzungs-Zug 501
Bekleidungs-Instandsetzungs-Zug 502
At the end of 1944 these platoons were fully motorised.

### Note:
1. V.Bl.d.W.-SS. Nr.7, 1 April 1945.

**Knöpfe**
Buttons

**Metal** (aluminium or zink, and later steel)

| | Flat-domed, hollow back | Flat-domed, shell | 4 hole fly | Aluminium/silver painted | Field-grey painted | Dark-grey painted | Black painted | White painted | Sand painted | Field-grey | Blue grey | Black | White | Grey (Fibre colour) |
|---|---|---|---|---|---|---|---|---|---|---|---|---|---|---|
| 1. 19 mm short shank (kurze Oese) | | — | — | — | — | — | — | — | — | | | | | |
| 2. 19 mm long shank | | — | — | — | | | | | | | | | | |
| 3. 19 mm channel back (Schlitzöse) | | — | — | — | | | | | | | | | | |
| 4. 16 mm short shank | — | — | — | — | — | — | — | | | | | | | |
| 5. 16 mm long shank | | — | — | — | | | | | | | | | | |
| 6. 16 mm screw back (Schraubknopf) | | — | — | — | — | | | | | | | | | |
| 7. 12 mm short shank | — | — | — | — | | | | | | | | | | |
| 8. 12 mm split pin (Splint) | | — | — | — | | | | | — | | | | | |
| 9. 15 mm fly | | | | — | | | | | | | | | | |

**Plastic fibre**

| | Flat-domed, hollow back | Flat-domed, shell | 4 hole fly | Aluminium/silver painted | Field-grey painted | Dark-grey painted | Black painted | White painted | Sand painted | Field-grey | Blue grey | Black | White | Grey (Fibre colour) |
|---|---|---|---|---|---|---|---|---|---|---|---|---|---|---|
| 10. 22 mm plastic | | | — | | | | | | | — | — | | — | |
| 11. 15 mm plastic | | | — | | | | | | | — | — | | | |
| 12. 15 mm fibre | | | — | | | | | | | | | | | — |

## General note

All German metal buttons had a pebbled or grained finish (gekörnt) which was designed primarily to avoid light reflection, and to prevent the painted finish from chipping off.

Shoulder strap buttons with arabic numerals to denote company, and roman to denote battalion were used in the SS-VT/Waffen-SS, but never as extensively as in the army.

In 1943 there was an attempt to introduce a standard button colour for all branches of the armed forces (previously the army had field-grey, navy, light grey and air-force, blue grey). The colour adopted was a dark bluish grey, and buttons painted this colour were designated standard buttons (Einheitsknöpfe).

Buttons were usually machine-sewn onto the uniforms, but on tropical and drill clothing which required frequent washing the buttons were removed by means of a split ring (Sprengringe/Splintringe).

# BIBLIOGRAPHY

Beadle, C. and Hartmann, T., WAFFEN-SS, ITS DIVISIONAL INSIGNIA, Key Publications, Bromley 1971.

DAMALS, ERINNERUNGEN AN GROSSE TAGE DER SS-TOTENKOPF-DIVISION IM FRANZÖSISCHEN FELDZUG 1940. Chr. Belser Verlag, Stuttgart 1940.

DAS SCHWARZE KORPS, ZEITUNG DER SCHUTZSTAFFEL DER NSDAP, ORGAN DER REICHSFÜHRUNG-SS, 1935–1945. Franz Eher, München.

DER FREIWILLIGE, KAMERADSCHAFTSBLATT DER HILFSGEMEIN-SCHAFT DER SOLDATEN DER EHEMALIGEN WAFFEN-SS, 1955–1972, Munin-Verlag, Osnabrück.

Der Reichszeugmeister, MITTEILUNGSBLATT DER REICHSZEUGMEI-STEREI DER NSDAP, 1933–1945, München.

DER SOLDATENFREUND, TASCHENJAHRBUCH FÜR DIE WEHRMACHT MIT KALENDARIUM FÜR 1944, Ausgabe D:Waffen-SS, 24. Jahrgang, Abgeschlossen mit dem 1 August 1943. Adolf Sponholz Verlag Hannover.

DEUTSCHE UNIFORMEN-ZEITSCHRIFT (incorporating Schwert und Spaten and Uniformen-Markt), 1943–1945. Uniformen-Markt, Berlin.

FELDGRAU, MITTEILUNGEN EINER ARBEITSGEMEINSCHAFT, Burgdorf/Hann., 1953–1966. Became Zeitschrift für neuzeitliche Wehrgeschichte in 1967. Die Ordens-Sammlung Berlin.

FM-ZEITSCHRIFT, Monatschrift der Reichsführung-SS für Fördernde Mitglieder, Berlin 1934–(?).

Fosten, D. F. V. and Marrion, R. J., WAFFEN-SS. Almark Publishing Co. Ltd., London 1971.

Georg, Enno, DIE WIRTSCHAFTLICHEN UNTERNEHMUNGEN DER SS, Deutsche Verlagsanstalt, Stuttgart 1963.

Gruder, E. DER DIENSTUNTERRICHT IM HEERE, AUSGABE FÜR DEN NACHRICHTENSOLDATEN. E. S. Mittler & Sohn, Berlin 1939.

Hausser, Paul, SOLDATEN WIE ANDERE AUCH, DER WEG DER WAFFEN-SS, Munin-Verlag GMBH, Osnabrück 1966.

Inspektion der SS-Verfügungstruppe, VERORDNUNGSBLATT DER IN-SPEKTION (E)DER SS-VERFÜGUNGSTRUPPE, April-May 1940 (3 issues) then became Verordnungsblatt der Waffen-SS.

Kanis, K, WAFFEN-SS IM BILD. Plesse Verlag, Göttingen 1957.

Keegan, John, WAFFEN-SS, THE ASPHALT SOLDIERS. Macdonald & Co. (Publishers) Ltd., London 1970.

Klietmann, K. G., DIE WAFFEN-SS, EINE DOKUMENTATION. Verlag 'Der Freiwillige' GMBH., Osnabrück 1965.

Krätschmer, Ernst-Günther, DIE RITTERKREUZTRÄGER DER WAFFEN-SS (2. Auflage) Plesse Verlag, Göttingen 1957.

Mollo, Andrew, UNIFORMS OF THE SS, VOL. 3, SS-VERFÜGUNGSTRUPPE 1933–39. Historical Research Unit, London 1970.

Mollo, Andrew, UNIFORMS OF THE SS, VOL. 4, SS-TOTENKOPFVER-BÄNDE 1933–1945. Historical Research Unit, London 1971.

Oberkommando des Heeres, HEERES-VERORDNUNGSBLATT (HVBL.) 1918–1945. Reichsdruckerei Berlin.

Oberkommando des Heeres, ALLGEMEINE HEERESMITTEILUNGEN(AHM) 1933–1945. Reichsdruckrei Berlin.

PICTURE HISTORY OF THE WAFFEN-SS. McLachlen Associates 1968.

Personalabteilung des Reichsführers-SS, DIENSTALTERLISTE DER SCHUTZ STAFFEL DER NSDAP.
Stand vom     1 Oktober 1934.
    ,,          1 Juli 1935.
    ,,          1 Dezember 1936.
    ,,          1 Dezember 1938.
    ,,          30 Januar 1942.
    ,,          20 April 1942
    ,,          1 Oktober 1942 (SS-Ostubaf.-SS-Stubaf.)
    ,,          9 November 1942 (SS-Obst.-Gru.-SS-Gruf.)
    ,,          30 Januar 1944 (SS-Obst.-Gruf.-SS-Staf.)
    ,,          1 Juli 1944 (SS-Ogruf.-SS-Hstuf.)
    ,,          1 Oktober 1944 (SS-Ostubaf.-SS-Stubaf.)

Reichsführer-SS, VORSCHRIFT ÜBER DIE BEKLEIDUNGSWIRTSCHAFT DER SS-VT. (BV-SS-TV) SS-Dienstvorschrift Nr.23. Berlin, March 1936.

Reichsführer-SS (SS-Hauptamt), DICH RUFT DIE SS. Verlag Hermann Hillger K.-G. Berlin-Grunewald und Leipzig 1943.

Schreiber, Franz, KAMPF UNTER DEM NORDLICHT, Munin Verlag GmbH, Osnabrück 1969.

Schutzstaffel der NSDAP, Kleiderkasse, PREISLISTE, Gültig ab 1 November 1940.

SCHWERT UND SPATEN, DIE ÄLTESTE DEUTSCHE FACHZEITSCHRIFT DER GESAMTEN AUSRÜSTUNGS-INDUSTRIE FUR HEER, LUFT-FAHRT, MARINE, ARBEITSDIENST, EINSCHLÄGEGE ORGANI-SATIONEN UND VERBÄNDE, 1932–1943. Scholz-Druck, Berlin.

SS-Führungshauptamt, SS-BEFEHLS-BLATT, 1933–1941. Berlin-Wilmersdorf.

SS-Führungshauptamt, VERORDNUNGSBLATT DER WAFFEN-SS (V.Bl.d.W.-SS), April 1940–April 1945, Berlin-Wilmersdorf.

Stein, George H, THE WAFFEN-SS, HITLER'S ELITE GUARD AT WAR, 1939–1945. Cornell University Press, Ithaca, New York 1966.

TASCHENBUCH FÜR DEN WINTERKRIEG, GEKÜRZTE AUSGABE VOM 1 September 1942. Erich Zander Druck- und Verlagshaus, Berlin.

THE SS IN BATTLE, A PHOTO ALBUM OF THE WAFFEN-SS IN COMBAT 1940–1945. McLachlen Associates 1969.

UNIFORMEN-MARKT, Fachzeitung der gesamten Uniformen-, Effekten-, Fahnen-, Paramenten-, Orden und Ehrenzeichen für Heer und Marine, Wehr-und Sportverbände 1934–1943. Otto Dietrich Verlag, Berlin.

UNIFORMS ORGANISATION AND HISTORY OF THE WAFFEN-SS, Vol. 1, R. J. Bender & H. P. Taylor. California 1969, Vol. 2, R. J. Bender & H. P. Taylor, California 1971.

Verwaltungsamt-SS, BEKLEIDUNGS-VORSCHRIFT FÜR DIE SCHUTZ-STAFFELN DER NSDAP (BV-SS) SS-Dienstvorschrift Nr.17, Berlin, Dezember 1934.

Walther, Herbert, DIE WAFFEN-SS EINE BILDDOKUMENTATION. L. B. Ahnert-Verlag, Echzell-Bisses 1971.

War Department, HANDBOOK ON GERMAN MILITARY FORCES (TM-E 30-451), 1 March 1945. Military Intelligence Division, Washington 1945.

War Office, HANDBOOK OF GERMAN ADMINISTRATION AND SUPPLY 1944. The War Office, April 1944.

Weidinger, Otto, DIVISION DAS REICH, Band 1, 1934–1939, Band 2, 1940–1941. Munin-Verlag GMBH, Osnabrück 1967.

Windrow, Martin, WAFFEN-SS, Osprey Men-at-Arms Series, Osprey Publishing Ltd, Reading 1971.

Zschäckel, Friedrich, WAFFEN-SS IM WESTEN, EIN BERICHT IN BILDERN VON SS-KRIEGSBERICHTER FRIEDRICH ZSCHÄCKEL, SS-PK. Franz Eher, München 1941.

## ERRATA & ADDENDA (Second Edition)

Page  4   Right column, line 15: for 'part 10' read 'page 10'.

Page  9   Right column, lines 30 & 33: for 'bad' read 'worn'.

Page  13  Left column, line 4: for 'any' read 'much'.
There is a photograph of Leon Degrelle wearing the Army-pattern metal Edelweiss on the left side of his boat-shaped field cap.

Page  27  The British captain wears the formation signs of the Royal Artillery of 15th (Scottish) Division.

Page  29  Sepp Dietrich is shaking hands with SS-Ostubaf. Mohnke. Directly behind Dietrich is Karl-Heinz Prinz; and, with fur collar, Dr. Gatternig.

Page  43  Caption: members of the SS-Heimwehr Danzig shown here are not wearing special SS pattern 'straps supporting', but the straps supplied with the metal load-bearing frame used by light mortar crews.

Page  44  The camouflage drill uniform made of unbleached twill was also manufactured in the 1944 'battledress' pattern: an example surfaced in a private collection in Vienna in 1976.

Page  49  Caption: the officer seated at the right is Aloys 'Luis' Schintlholzer.

Page  58  Add to end of first paragraph: It would appear from the photograph on page 224 of Otto Weidinger's 'DIVISION DAS REICH IM BILD' that at least one armoured car crew obtained Luftwaffe leather two-piece winter flying suits.

Page  61  Notes: insert '4. See illustration on this page.'
Line 15 et seq: Since publication of the first edition little new information on special clothing for SS parachute troops has come to light. An American collector sent me a photograph of a pair of field-grey trousers, identical to the Luftwaffe pattern but bearing a label with an SS contract number. I am doubtful about the authenticity of camouflage trousers published in colour photographs in *Military Illustrated* magazine (No. 31, December 1990). These seem to be an exact copy of the field-grey trousers. If such trousers had been mass produced they would be of a professional standard; but if made by an individual or at unit level they would probably have been simplified, and made from materials to hand rather than from camouflage herringbone twill, which would only have been available from SS clothing factories or textile depots.

With regard to the national emblem being worn on the right breast of Waffen-SS uniforms: the late Richard Schulze-Kossens sent me a photograph of an SS officer wearing the Army national emblem on the right breast of his Waffen-SS tunic. A group photograph in this author's collection shows the 1st Replacement (Ersatz) Company of Infantry Regiment 75, under the command of SS-Untersturmführer Geletneky, who wears SS-Verfügungstruppe uniform without the SS national emblem on the sleeve but with the Army one on the right Greast.

It has been suggested that a reason for wearing the SS national emblem on the right breast of the parachute smock was that both Luftwaffe and Waffen-SS rank badges for uniforms without shoulder straps were worn on the upper sleeves.

Page  66  Caption: the officer in winter clothing is SS-Hauptsturmführer Hans-Georg Charpentier, who was awarded the Ritterkreuz on 29 December 1942.
SS parkas made from Italian camouflage material with front button fastening were found in Dachau at the end of the war.

Page  67  Line 5: should read 'possibly Riga'.

Page  77  Left column, lines 6-8: the rank designations Staffel-Anwärter, Staffelmann and Staffel-Sturmann were discontinued. See V.Bl.d.W-SS, Nr.10, 18 July 1941, Ziff.293.

Page  78  Right column: add to list of rank designations:
SS-Nachschubkommandanturen — SS-Schütze — SS-Oberschütze.
See Microfilm Series RFSS T-175 109/3735, dated 20 March 1942.

Page  79  Line 11: add 'For a short period, three stars were worn on the shoulder straps when rank collar patches were not being worn. See Volume 7 of the present series, page 54.'
Replace Para 22 with the following:
On 7 April 1942 Hitler approved the introduction of a new SS rank of SS-Oberstgruppenführer (later hyphenated thus: SS-Oberst-Gruppenführer, to avoid confusion with the rank of SS-Obergruppenführer). Himmler put forward Sepp Dietrich's name as the first recipient of this rank; but since Dietrich was only a divisional commander, and an SS Corps did not yet exist, Hitler demurred in deference to anticipated Army displeasure. On 23 June 1943 Hitler honoured Dietrich with the unique rank designation of SS-Obergruppenführer und Panzergeneral der Waffen-

SS, in recognition of his status as senior active tank man at the front. In the spring of 1944 the I SS-Panzerkorps became operational; but it was not until 23 August 1944 that Dietrich began to wear the rank badges of an SS-Oberst-Gruppenführer und Panzer-Generaloberst der Waffen-SS.

*Notes*: add '5a. Microfilm Series RFSS T-175 105/8086 dated 31 October 1941.'

Note 10: I have been unable to recover the missing footnote.

Note 17: for 'two' read 'three'.

Page 90 Line 1: title should read 'DIENSTGRADABZEICHEN'.

Page 91 The photograph on the left shows the Swedish SS-Standartenoberjunker Hans Caspar Krüger, wearing on the left breast pocket the Swedish badge for Military Field Sports in gold above the Skiing Badge. He died in Buenos Aires in 1977.

The photograph on the right was taken at Tergensee in August 1944.

Page 102 Caption: the black overalls were also worn by tank crews in action.

Page 103 Right column, line 4: officers retained the Waffenfarbe of their former unit.

Line 6: read 'Stamm der Junker und Unterführerschulen'.

Line 14: read 'Artillerie-Schulen I u.II'.

Page 104 Right column, line 19: read '...u. Nachrichten)'.

Page 105 Left column, line 12: see Microfilm Series RFSS T-175 110/4630 dated 17 July 1941.

Second column, line 4: read 'SS-Hauptämtern'.

Right column, line 17: read 'Personlicher Stab der RFSS'.

Right column, after line 21: add 'SS-Jägerbataillone 500-502'. See Zeitschrift für Heereskunde, Nr.302/3, Jul/Okt 1982, pp. 124–5.

Page 107 Caption: according to the late Dr. K. G. Klietmann the wearing of the lanyard by Unterführer vom Dienst was unique to the Leibstandarte. Letter to the author dated 25 January 1973. Also: for 'practise' read 'practice'.

Page 129 After line 7: a label found on a field-grey herringbone twill Sturmartillerie jacket suggests that there was also a Bekleidungswerk in Posen (Poznan).

Page 132 Right column, between lines 25 & 26, add the following edition of the SS-Dienstalterliste: 15 May 1943 (SS-Obst.-Gruf. – SS-Staf.)

Page 133 Left column, line 3: read 'Einschlagige'.

Line 14: add 'Gaithersburg, Maryland'.

# SS CAMOUFLAGE PATTERNS

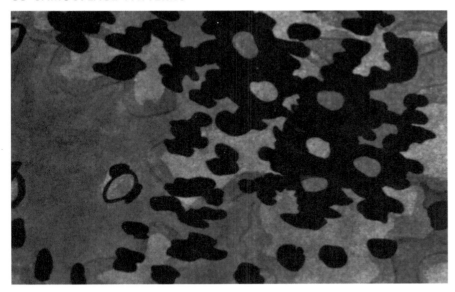

Typical summer and autumn patterns found on waterproof cotton duck.

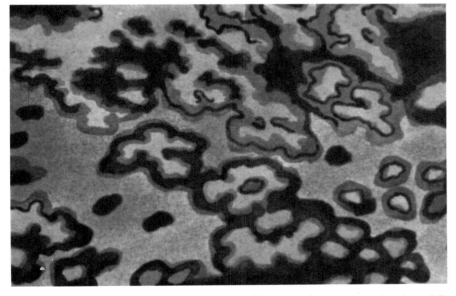

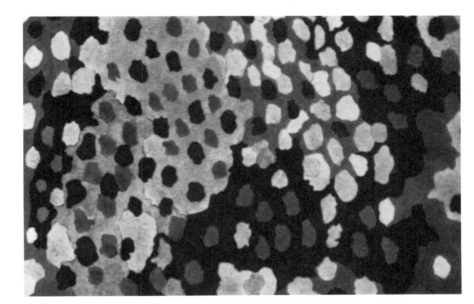

Autumn pattern found on the winter combat uniform, and final pattern printed on drill material.